Emotional Intelligence

Journey to Self-Positive

EMOTIONAL INTELLIGENCE

Journey to Self-Positive

Pooja V. Anand
Assistant Professor, Department of Psychology
Daulat Ram College, University of Delhi
Delhi - 110007

The Readers Paradise
New Delhi

Emotional Intelligence – Journey to Self-Positive

ISBN - 978-93-85958-62-5
1st Edition

Published by
The Readers Paradise
103, 4787/23, Ansari Road,
Darya Ganj, New Delhi - 110002
011-23246222, 09811197091, 9654444181
thereaderspparadisesales@gmail.com
www.thereadersparadise.com

Typsetting by
Sanya Computers, Bhajanpura

Cover Design
Kamini Bijoria, Daryaganj, New Delhi - 110002

Printed in India
Balaji Offset, Naveen Shahadara

Price - Rs. 495.00 Size - 5.5"X8.5"
Pages - 133 Paper - 80gsm

Contents

To

My Dear Daughter Nemo

Acknowledgments

The topic of emotional intelligence has always been close to my heart since I was a college student. When I first came across this topic I found myself curiously and passionately drawn towards it. Since then most of my research has been on emotional intelligence including my PhD. Working on emotional intelligence for more than almost a decade and a half now, I always dreamt of putting my own thoughts and ideas related to it in a book but didn't really pursue my dream unless I got motivation from an unexpected source!

Three years back seeing me reading a book intently and noting important points, my then three years old daughter Nemo with her utmost childhood innocence remarked "Mumma why are you reading this book and underlining, instead you should write your own book, which others will read and underline!"

Needless to say, I was pleasantly surprised and overjoyed by those innocent yet really meaningful words! Those beautiful words reignited my dream of writing my own book on emotional intelligence! I can't thank my daughter enough for motivating me to pursue my dream! This book is dedicated to you Nemo!

This book would not have been possible without the contant motivation and support of my husband, Virender. My husband has always been my pillar of strength. He is more ambitious for me and more confident about my abilities than I ever could be about myself. I'm blessed to have such a wonderful, loving, and supportive life partner.

I would like to thank all my family members for always believing in me and motivating me to reach new heights in my career and life.

My sincere gratitude to Prof. N. K. Chadha for writing the foreword for this book and for always encouraging and motivating me.

The dream of getting my book published would not have been fulfilled without the cooperation and enthusiastic support of my publisher, The Readers Paradise. I thank them profusely for helping me in fulfilling my dream.

Above all, I thank the Almighty for everything that I have been blessed with.

Preface

Traditionally emotions have been viewed as irrational and considered as secondary to logic and reason. However, with the emergence of the topic of emotional intelligence towards the end of the twentieth century, there has been a renewed focus on the topic of emotions. Emotions are now looked upon as facilitating thought, and making life colourful and meaningful. The concept of emotional intelligence involves understanding and managing one's own and others' emotions as well as using one's emotional energy to attain a positive self.

Ever since work on emotional intelligence started, numerous research articles and books have been published on it. However, most of the books centre on a particular context like school or the workplace. Many books are self-help books. In this sense there is a paucity of textbooks on this topic, which provide a detailed understanding of the construct of emotional intelligence.

The present book entitled *Emotional Intelligence–Journey to Self-positive* has been written with the aim to provide a comprehensive text to give a detailed understanding of the topic of emotional intelligence. The book has been divided into nine chapters each covering a core aspect of emotional intelligence.

Chapter 1 gives a brief account of the topic of emotions and the important theories of emotions. *Chapter 2* discusses the long journey of the emergence and growth of the construct of emotional intelligence. It details the contribution of various theorists in shaping the concept of emotional intelligence. *Chapter 3* gives a detailed account of the various models and definitions of emotional intelligence. It simultaneously discusses the various measures of emotional intelligence based on these models. *Chapter 4* describes briefly the Indian view of emotional intelligence and the work done by Indian researchers on emotional intelligence.

Chapter 5 illustrates the importance of emotional intelligence in various domains of life with the help of research done in this area. *Chapter 6* discusses emotional intelligence as a competency that can be learned in view of research evidence. *Chapter 7* gives an account of the controversies and criticisms surrounding the construct of emotional intelligence. *Chapter 8* introduces and discusses a new model of emotional intelligence developed by the author called the 3S model of emotional intelligence. *Chapter 9* concludes the text by presenting a strong case for emotional intelligence and the importance of integrating it in school and college curricula.

In all, this book aims to provide a detailed account of all aspects of emotional intelligence. This book presents comprehensive material to give the reader a complete understanding of the construct of emotional intelligence and its related aspects. Figures are presented at various places to enhance the understanding of the topics. The book also provides strategies for enhancing emotional intelligence.

One of the most important features of the book is that it provides a new model called the *3S model of emotional intelligence* developed by the author. The model is quite comprehensive and describes the important components of emotional intelligence. The model is based on years of research on emotional intelligence by the author with various samples. This textbook on emotional intelligence has been written in a way that is informative as well as interesting to read. I hope the readers enjoy reading the book as much as I have enjoyed writing it!

Author

Foreword

Emotional intelligence has become one of the most important constructs in recent social science literature today. This is due to the fact that the applications of emotional intelligence have been found in many areas of human development and excellence with focused application to achieve National as well as International goals. Apart from this, emotional intelligence has many applications in business and management as well. Given the importance of emotional intelligence in all walks of life and psychology in particular, it is quite essential that not only professionals and school children but undergraduate and postgraduate students in social science develop a keen understanding of emotional intelligence.

Many popular books have been written on emotional intelligence. However, there is a dearth of academic books on emotional intelligence. Given how important the construct and its understanding is in today's world, it is of prime importance that good textbooks are written on emotional intelligence.

The book "Emotional Intelligence-Journey to Self-Positive" makes an important contribution in this direction. It is one of the first textbooks to be written on emotional intelligence. The book contains detailed reading material on the topic of emotional intelligence. The book has been divided into nine chapters that cover various important facets related to emotional intelligence. Chapter 1 provides an introduction to the topic of emotions. Chapter 2 outlines the development of the construct of emotional intelligence. Chapter 3 details the important models and measures of emotional intelligence. Chapter 4 provides the Indian view of emotional intelligence. Chapter 5 discusses the importance of emotional intelligence. Chapter 6 describes how emotional intelligence is a competency that can be learnt. Chapter 7 discusses various issues related to emotional intelligence. Chapter 8 discusses a new model of emotional intelligence developed and tested by Dr Pooja V. Anand, the author of this book. Chapter 9 provides a brief summary of the book by outlining the importance of emotional intelligence.

The book provides comprehensive reading material on the topic of emotional intelligence that can benefit both undergraduate and post-graduate students in psychology as well as students in management. By authoring this book, Dr Pooja V. Anand has fulfilled an urgent need for a textbook on the topic of emotional intelligence. I'm sure this book will be very well received not only by students and teachers in psychology but by academicians in other social sciences as well. My best wishes for the success of this book!

I feel honoured to write the foreword of this book and congratulate the author, Dr. Pooja V. Anand as well the publisher The Readers Paradise to make such an attempt. The book is worth reading and possessing.

Prof. Dr. N.K. Chadha
Chairperson (Research and Doctoral Program)
Manav Rachna International University
Former, Prof. and Head, Department of Psychology,
University of Delhi
Former, Chairman, Board of Research in Humanities
and Social Sciences, University of Delhi

1

Introduction to Emotions

> *"The emotional intelligence field is on the steep incline of a new wave of understanding–how people can improve their EQ and make lasting gains that have a profoundly positive impact upon their lives" (Bradberry & Greaves, 2009, p. 9).*

Emotional intelligence has become a very popular topic in today's world. Emotional intelligence was declared as one of the most useful phrases of the late 1990s by the American Dialect Society (Mayer, Salovey & Caruso, 2000). Many books have been published and many articles have been written on emotional intelligence. Researchers all over the globe are researching on it. Emotional intelligence has caught the attention of both academia and the public. Throughout the world various conferences are being held to discuss and debate this interesting area of research. Many schools have started training programs in emotional skills. In business emotional intelligence is growing into a huge training industry. Many of the major newspapers and magazines of the world have published articles on emotional intelligence. Therefore, it can be seen that emotional intelligence has really become a major topic of interest worldwide. Before discussing the topic of emotional intelligence in detail, let us briefly overview the basic concepts and theories related to emotions.

Emotions

Emotions are feeling (or affect) states that involve a pattern of cognitive, physiological, and behavioural reactions to events (Passer & Smith, 2011). Emotions serve many important functions, the most important being adaptation. For instance, fear helps in survival as it is part of the emergency arousal system. Positive emotions such as joy, love, etc. too have important adaptive functions. Positive emotions help us in broadening our thinking so that we explore new ideas and try out new ways to solve problems (Frederickson, 1998). Emotions also facilitate social communication. For example, when a baby cries the adults respond with love and care. In the same manner adults in distress receive help from others.

The Nature of Emotions (Passer & Smith, 2011)

1. **Stimuli:** Emotions are triggered by eliciting stimuli. They can be internal or external.
2. **Appraisal:** Emotional responses result from our appraisal of stimuli. This helps in giving the situation its perceived meaning and significance.
3. **Physiological response:** There is a physiological response

of our bodies to the appraisals. Many parts of the body are involved in emotional arousal. Certain brain regions, such as limbic system and cerebral cortex, the autonomic nervous system, and the endocrine system play an important role in emotions.

4. **Behaviour tendencies:** Emotions include behaviour tendencies. Some are expressive behaviours (eg. crying) whereas others are instrumental behaviours, which are the ways of doing something about the stimulus that evolved the emotion (eg studying for a test that evokes anxiety).

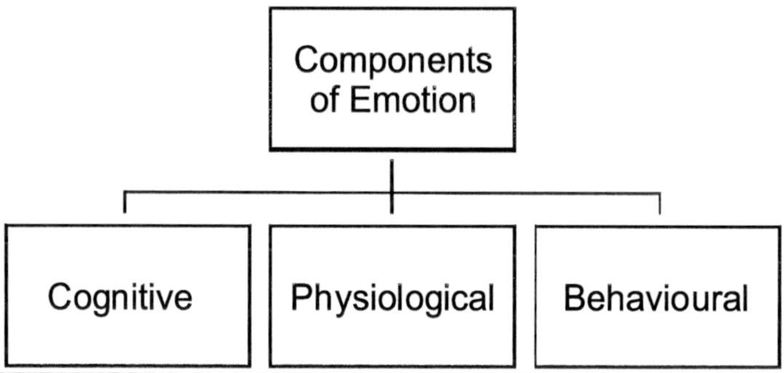

Figure 1.1 – Components of emotion

Universality of Emotional Expression

In his classic book *The Expression of Emotions in Man and Animals* (1872/1965) Darwin stated that since emotional displays contribute to species survival, they are products of evolution. Likewise, modern evolutionary theorists stress the adaptive value of emotional expression (Izard, 1989; Plutchik,

1994). These theorists believe that some fundamental emotional patterns, or innate emotional reactions, are wired into our nervous system (Panksepp, 2005).

Most of us are quite confident regarding our ability to read the emotions of others. In communicating feelings various parts of the body are involved. Yet we focus more on the face. Facial expressions provide valuable information for judging emotion.

There has been an ongoing controversy as to whether there are any facial expressions associated with emotions, which are universal for humans. Darwin (1872) proposed universal facial expression of emotions on the basis of his evolutionary theory. Allport (1924), Asch (1952), and Tomkins (1962, 1963) too favoured universal emotional facial behaviour. However, these researchers also recognized that there would be cultural differences in facial behaviour as well.

The role of culture has been found to be important in understanding various psychological phenomena. According to Ashforth and Humphrey (1995) 'Culture provides beliefs about emotional states, a vocabulary for discriminating them and a set of socially acceptable attributes for the states'. Cross-cultural research has suggested that the components of expression and regulation of emotion depend heavily on cultural context although some components of emotions are universal such as, appraisal and understanding of emotion (Ekman, 1992).

Ekman conducted significant research on biological

correlates of specific emotions and demonstrated the universality of emotions. He was interested in non-verbal communication and focussed on developing techniques for measuring non-verbal communication. Ekman and Freisen (1971) determined that there are six basic emotions that are expressed by certain facial expressions shared by people in all cultures. These basic emotions are: *anger, disgust, fear, happiness, sadness, and surprise*. Later research showed new evidence for the emotion of *contempt*, which is now commonly grouped with the original six basic emotions. Further studies during 1990s revealed new group of emotions that fit the criteria for basic emotions: *guilt, shame, interest, embarrassment, awe, and excitement* (Ekman, 1992). According to Friesen (1972) facial expression of emotion is determined to a large extent by the cultural rule prevailing in the society.

Cultural display rules dictate when and how particular emotions are to be expressed (Yrizarry, Matsumoto, Imai, Kooken & Takeuchi, 2001). Certain gestures, body postures, and physical movements may have different meanings in different cultures.

Theories of Emotion

The James-Lange theory

William James (1890) wrote:

Common sense says... we meet a bear, are frightened,

and run; we are insulted by a rival, are angry, and strike. The hypothesis here to be defended says that this order of sequence is incorrect and that the more rational statement is that we feel sorry because we cry, angry because we strike, afraid because we tremble. (James, 1890/1950, p. 451)

Around the same time, Carl Lange stated a similar argument. Hence, according to this theory, our bodily reactions determine the subjective emotion we experience. Feedback from the body's reactions to a situation tells the brain that we are experiencing an emotion. With such feedback, an emotional response is generated.

The Cannon-Bard Theory

In 1927, Walter Cannon challenged the James-Lange theory. Cannon and his colleague L. L. Bard proposed their theory of emotion. According to this theory, the subjective experience of emotion and physiological arousal do not cause one another. They are rather independent responses to an emotion-arousing situation. Emotional experiences occur due to signals sent directly from the thalamus to the cortex, not from bodily feedback.

Cognitive-affective Theories

Cognitive-affective theories focus on the interaction between cognitions and physiological responses. Lazarus (2001) argued that all emotional responses require some sort of appraisal. According to Schachter's two-factor theory of emotion, the intensity of physiological arousal tells us how strongly we are feeling something but, situational cues provide us the information we need to label the arousal and tell ourselves what we are feeling – fear, anger, love, or some other emotion (Schachter, 1966).

□□□

2

Emergence and Growth of the Construct of Emotional Intelligence

Emotions and its related aspects have been areas of research interest since a long time and many researchers have attempted to research on them and understand their functioning. Traditionally emotions were considered to be of lesser value. They were viewed as disrupting the ability to reason and think. Greater importance was given to rationality and logic. However, with the upsurge in the study of emotions now, the view has changed wherein emotions are now viewed as quite important in facilitating thought. It is also being largely understood now that the dichotomy between emotion and reason is redundant.

In this regard the work of Charles Darwin in the 19th century is of great importance. Since the publication of his book *The Expression of Emotions in Man and Animals* in 1872, a lot of interest was generated in the topic of emotions.

In 1920, E. L. Thorndike proposed the concept of social intelligence. Thorndike (1920) defined social intelligence as "the ability to understand and manage men and women, boys and girls to act wisely in human relations" (p. 228). Social intelligence also includes the ability to understand and manage oneself. Hence, the concept of social intelligence helped in the emergence of the construct of emotional intelligence.

Wechsler (1944) defined intelligence as "the aggregate or global capacity of the individual to act purposefully, to think rationally, and to deal effectively with his environment" (p. 3). He proposed that the non-intellective abilities are crucial for predicting one's ability to succeed in life as well as adaptation. By "non-intellective" he meant affective, personal, and social factors.

The Ohio State Leadership Studies conducted in the 1940s under the guidance of Hemphill found that "consideration" is crucial to effective leadership. It was found that leaders who are successful in establishing mutual trust, respect, warmth and rapport with members of their group are more effective. Around the same time, the Office of Strategic Services developed a process of assessment, which included evaluation of cognitive as well as non-cognitive abilities. This later evolved into the assessment centre. Many of the dimensions measured by assessment centres involve social and emotional competencies. In the late 1940s, a lot of research was carried out on *alexithymia,* which focuses on the inability to recognise, understand and describe emotions.

The Sommerville study was a 40 year longitudinal study of 450 boys who grew up in Sommerville, Massachusetts (Cherniss, 2000). Two-thirds of the boys were from welfare families, and one-third had IQ's below 90. It was found that IQ played little role in determining how well the boys did in their lives. Rather the biggest difference amongst these boys was made by abilities such as being able to handle frustration, control emotions, and getting along with other people.

In the late 1960s and early 1970s the "marshmallow studies" were conducted at Stanford University led by psychologist Walter Mischel. Four year olds were asked to stay in a room alone with a marshmallow and wait for a researcher to return. They were told that if they waited until the researcher came back before eating the marshmallow, they could have two. Ten years later the researchers studied the kids who participated in the study. They found that the kids who were able to resist temptation had a total SAT score, which was 210 points higher than those kids who were unable to wait (Shoda, Mischel & Peake, 1990).

In 1983, Gardner in his book *Frames of mind: The theory of multiple intelligences* introduced the idea of *multiple intelligences*. Among the various types of intelligences mentioned by him, two of them were quite close to the concept of emotional intelligence: intrapersonal and interpersonal. According to him, intrapersonal intelligence involves the capacity to understand oneself, appreciate one's feelings, motivating oneself etc. whereas interpersonal intelligence includes the ability to understand the emotions, and motivations of others. In Gardner's view, traditional type of intelligence fails to fully explain cognitive ability.

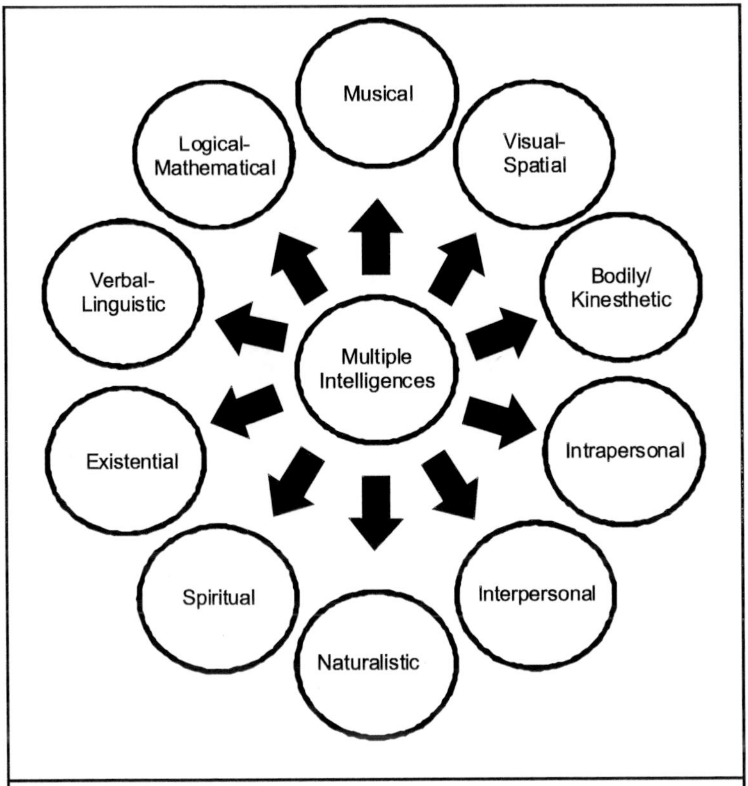

Figure 2.1 – Gardner's Multiple Intelligences

Sternberg (1985, 1991) proposed the Triarchic theory of intelligence with the following parts: Analytic intelligence, Creative intelligence and Practical intelligence. According to Sternberg, Analytic intelligence is the ability to analyze ideas, make decisions, and solve problems. Creative intelligence is the ability to adapt to changing environmental conditions and to shape the environment so as to maximize one's strength and compensate for one's weaknesses. He also introduced the concept of Practical intelligence, which is the ability to accomplish personally valued goals by adapting to the environment, shaping the environment or selecting a new environment. He argued that Practical intelligence is different from academic intelligence and can explain individual differences in performance beyond IQ. The first use of the term *emotional intelligence* was found in Payne's (1985) doctoral thesis: *A study of emotion: developing emotional intelligence.*

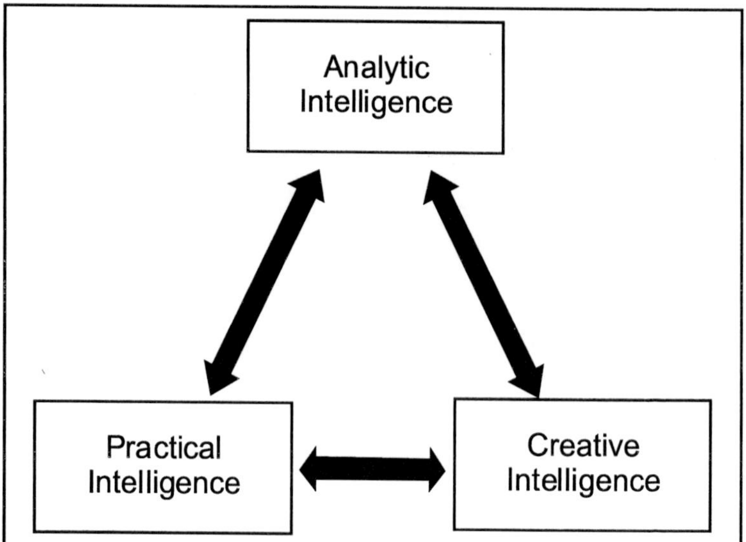

Figure 2.2 – Sternberg's Triarchic Theory of Intelligence

Salovey and Mayer coined the very term emotional intelligence in 1990 (Salovey & Mayer, 1990; Mayer & Salovey, 1993, 1995). In 1990, a review of literature was done (Salovey & Mayer, 1990) and a theory of emotional intelligence was developed. An editorial in the journal *Intelligence* (Mayer & Salovey, 1993) was published, which reiterated serious study in the area of emotional intelligence. Salovey and Mayer (1990) described emotional intelligence as "a form of social intelligence that involves the ability to monitor one's own and others' emotions, to discriminate among them, and to use the information to guide one's thinking and actions" (p.189).

Goleman authored the books *Emotional Intelligence: Why It Can Matter More Than IQ* (1995) and *Working with Emotional Intelligence (1998).* Goleman was a behavioural science writer for the New York Times, who wrote on brain and behaviour research. He was trained as a psychologist at Harvard where he worked with David McClelland, among others. McClelland found that the traditional tests of cognitive intelligence were limited in explaining as to what leads to success in life. For instance, IQ by itself is not a very good predictor of job performance. McClelland (1973) in his paper *Testing for Competence Rather than Intelligence* stressed the importance of competencies beyond the traditional concept of intelligence that lead to success.

Goleman (1995) made an interesting claim about the importance of emotional intelligence by stating that whereas IQ (Intelligence Quotient) contributes to only 20% of life success, 80% is done by EQ (Emotional Quotient). According to Goleman (1995) the contribution of emotional intelligence to effective performance at work is as much as 66 percent for all jobs and 85 percent for leadership jobs. Goleman (1998) discussed how EQ significantly contributes to success at school, home, and the workplace. He also stated that many negative behaviours like drug addiction, smoking, and bullying are inversely related to emotional intelligence.

Goleman popularized the concept of emotional intelligence and applied it in the context of work situation. Now emotional intelligence is considered as a better predictor of managerial success than the traditionally accepted concept of intelligence. As Goleman (1998) puts it "it is not that IQ and technical skills are irrelevant, they do matter but mainly as "threshold capabilities"; that is they are the entry level requirements for executive positions..." (p.94). Rather it is emotional intelligence that differentiates between those who perform at an outstanding level and those who work at a basic level of competence.

Goleman's (1998) book emphasized that effectiveness of employees, teams and the entire organization is influenced by emotional and social competencies. Gibbs' (1995) *Time* magazine article highlighted Goleman's book and was one of the first articles in the mainstream media on emotional intelligence. Thereafter, articles on emotional intelligence began to appear with increasing frequency. As the field was popularized, many definitions and models of emotional intelligence evolved. Goleman (1995) largely considered emotional intelligence as good social behaviour. Hence, with all this the concept of emotional intelligence was enlarged than what was there in the scientific literature.

Recently Bradberry and Greaves (2009) published a book named *Emotional Intelligence 2.0*. They defined emotional intelligence as "the ability to identify, consider and control emotions in oneself and to recognize them in others, brought on by a combination of self-awareness, self-management, social awareness and relationship management" (Bradberry & Greaves, 2009).

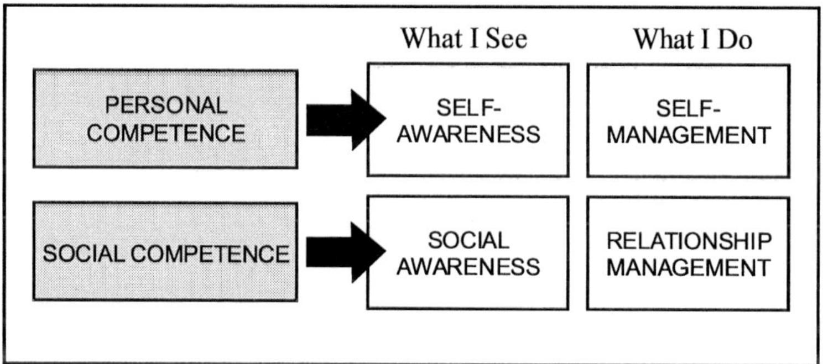

Figure 2.3 – Model of emotional intelligence

Adapted from Bradberry & Greaves (2009)

□□□

3

Models and Measures of Emotional Intelligence

According to the *"Encyclopaedia of Applied Psychology"*, there are three basic models of emotional intelligence: (a) the Salovey-Mayer model (b) the Goleman model, and (c) the Bar-On model. Mayer, Salovey and Caruso (2000) have classified emotional intelligence models under two categories:

1. The ability model proposed by Mayer and Salovey (1997).
2. The mixed model proposed mainly by Goleman (1998), Boyatzis, Goleman and Rhee (2000) and Bar-On (1997, 2000).

Salovey and Mayer's (1990), Mayer, Salovey, & Caruso's (2000) theory placed emotional intelligence within a model of intelligence wherein emotion and thought interact in meaningful and adaptive ways. Bar-On placed emotional intelligence in the context of personality theory and Goleman formulated emotional intelligence in terms of a theory of performance.

According to Mayer and Salovey (1997) and Salovey and Mayer (1990), the mixed models describe a kind of compound conception of intelligence that includes mental abilities, and other dispositions and traits. Mixed models treat mental abilities and a variety of other characteristics and social activity as a single entity (Bar On, 1997; Goleman, 1995).

1. The Ability Model of Emotional Intelligence

Salovey and Mayer's (1990) original model described emotional intelligence as "a form of social intelligence that involves the ability to monitor one's own and others' feelings and emotions, to discriminate among them, and to use this information to guide one's thinking and actions" (p. 189). Later they defined emotional intelligence as "the ability to perceive accurately, the appraisal and expression of emotions, the ability to access and/or generate feelings so as to assist thought, the ability to understand emotions and emotional knowledge, and the ability to regulate emotions so as to promote emotional and intellectual growth" (Mayer & Salovey, 1997). The four branch model of emotional intelligence describes four areas of capacities or skills that collectively describe many of areas of emotional intelligence (Mayer & Salovey, 1997).

The Four Branches of Emotional Intelligence (Mayer &Salovey, 1997)

1. **Perceiving Emotions:** The ability to perceive

emotions in oneself and others as well as in other stimuli.

2. **Facilitating Thought:** The ability to generate, use, and feel emotion as necessary to communicate feelings or use them in other cognitive processes.
3. **Understanding Emotions:** The ability to understand emotional information, to understand how emotions combine and progress through relationship transitions and to appreciate such emotional meanings.
4. **Managing Emotions:** The ability to be open to feelings and to modulate them in oneself and others so as to promote personal understanding and growth.

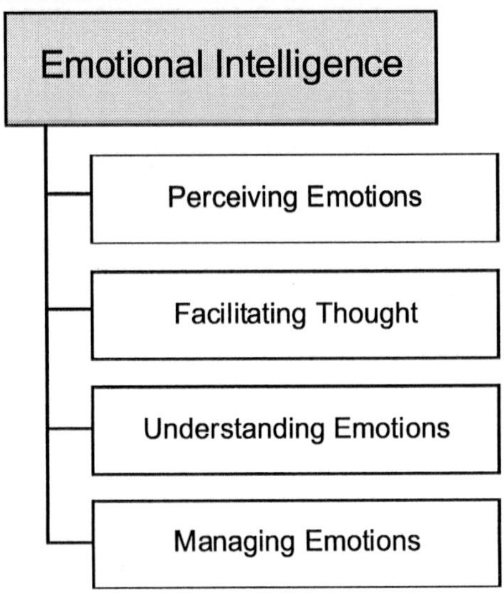

Figure 3.1 – Mayer and Salovey's Four Branch Model of Emotional Intelligence

The most important measures of emotional intelligence as ability are Multifactor Emotional Intelligence Scale (Mayer, Salovey & Caruso, 1997) and Mayer Salovey Caruso Emotional Intelligence Test (Mayer, Salovey & Caruso, 2002). The Multifactor Emotional Intelligence Scale (MEIS) (Mayer, Caruso & Salovey, 1999) consists of 12 scales, divided into four branches of abilities: (a) perceiving, (b) assimilating (c) understanding and (d) managing emotion. In the MEIS the respondent performs a series of tasks designed to assess the person's ability to perceive, identify, understand, and work with emotion.

The Mayer-Salovey-Caruso Emotional Intelligence Test (MSCEIT) measures how well people perform tasks and solve emotional problems. The MSCEIT was developed from the Multifactor Emotional Intelligence Scale (MEIS). It has 141 items and provides 15 main scores and three Supplemental scores. The MSCEIT has a factor structure congruent with the four-part model of emotional intelligence and it is both reliable and content valid. According to its authors the MSCEIT meets several standard criteria for a new intelligence: It is operationalized as a set of abilities and is objective; its scores correlate with existing intelligences while also showing unique variance; and scores increase with age (Mayer, Caruso, & Salovey, 1999; Mayer, Salovey, & Caruso, 2002; Mayer & Geher, 1996).

The MSCEIT Version 2.0 (Mayer, Salovey, & Caruso, 2002) contains 141 items. The test consists of eight tasks, which are divided into four branches of abilities. Three scores are obtained: a total EI score, and two area scores: Experiencing EI and a Strategic EI. Correct answers on the test are evaluated in terms of agreement with a general or expert consensus (Mayer, Salovey, & Caruso, 2002).

Table 3.1 Characteristics of an emotionally intelligent person (Based on Mayer, Salovey & Caruso, 2004)
➢ Can better perceive emotions
➢ Uses emotions in thought
➢ Understands the meaning of emotions
➢ Manages emotions for solving emotional problems
➢ Higher in verbal, social, and other intelligences
➢ More open and agreeable
➢ Drawn to occupations involving social interactions
➢ Less apt to engage in problem behaviours
➢ Avoids self-destructive, negative behaviours
➢ Has more positive social interactions
➢ More adept at describing motivational goals, aims, and missions
➢ Understands the full richness and complexities of communications
➢ Good at establishing positive social relationships with others
➢ Avoids conflicts, fights, and other social altercations
➢ Good at understanding psychologically healthy living
➢ Provides coaching advice to others
➢ Assists other individuals and groups of people to live together with greater harmony and satisfaction

2. Model of Emotional Social Intelligence

Bar-On prefers the term "emotional-social intelligence" to "emotional intelligence" or "social intelligence". Bar-On (2000) defined emotional intelligence in terms of "an array of emotional and social knowledge and abilities that influence the overall ability to effectively relate with environmental demands". It includes (a) the ability to be aware of, to understand and to express oneself; (b) the ability to be aware of, to understand and to relate to others (3) the ability to deal with strong emotions and control one's impulses and (4) the ability to adapt to change and to solve problems of a personal or social nature, and general mood.

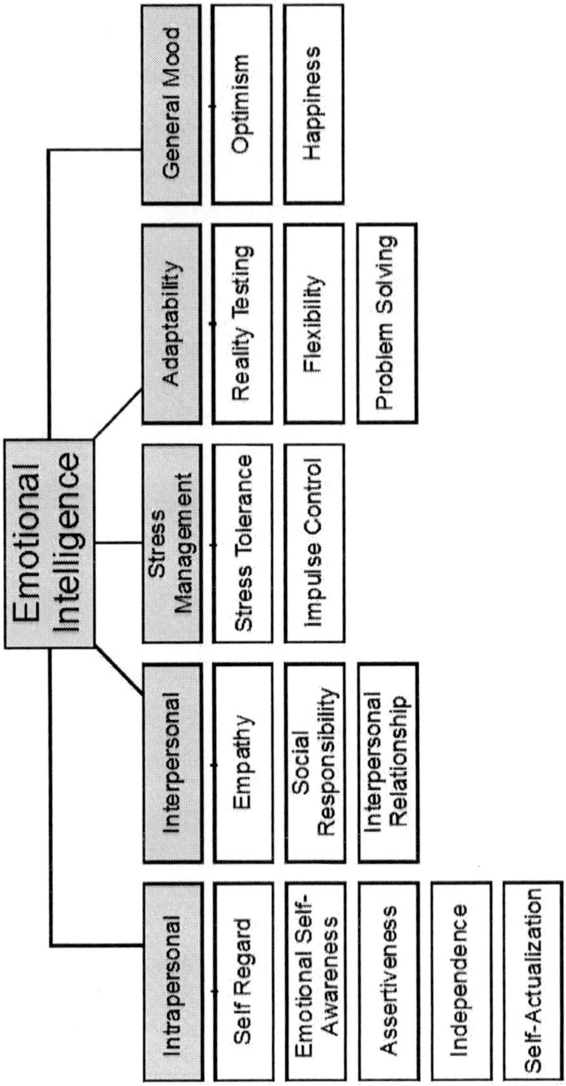

Figure 3.2

Bar-On's Model of Emotional Social Intelligence

Bar-On developed a measure of emotional intelligence that used the term Emotional Quotient (EQ). Bar-On developed a general measure of social and emotional intelligence that predicts emotional well-being and adaptation. The EQ-i (Bar-On, 1997) is a self-report measure of Emotional Social Intelligence that evolved out of the questions, "Why do some people have better psychological well-being than others?; and why are some people able to succeed in life over others?" (Bar-On, 1997, p. 1). The EQ-i is suitable for individuals 17 years of age and older. The five main domains in this measure are interpersonal skills, interpersonal skills, adaptability, stress management, and general mood. The EQ-i is a paper and pencil test that has 133 brief items and a 5-point Likert type scale. It gives an overall EQ score as well as scores for the following 5 composite scales and 15 subscales:-

- Interpersonal (Self-Regard, Emotional Self-Awareness, Assertiveness, Independence and Self-Actualization)
- Interpersonal (Empathy, Social Responsibility, and Interpersonal Relationship)
- Stress Management (Stress Tolerance and Impulse Control)
- Adaptability (Reality Testing, Flexibility and Problem Solving)
- General Mood Scale (Optimism and Happiness)

Recently Bar-On (2000) made a revision to his scale; he

now views the general mood factor as a facilitator of emotional intelligence rather than a part of it. Thus, total EQ-i scores are now computed by only summing the first four scales.

Bar-On EQ-i ® has four validity indices and a correction factor. Considerable research has been done about its reliability, convergent and discriminant validity. Recent studies have shown that the EQ-i correlates strongly with a number of personality measures, including Neuroticism on the Big Five, anxiety on the 16PF, depression with the BDI, and alexythymia (Dawda & Hart, 2000; Parker, Taylor, & Bagby, 2001). The Bar-On EQ-i YV is a self-report instrument designed to measure emotional intelligence in young people. The test uses a four point Likert type scale. Reliability coefficients for the 15 subscales that comprise the factor scores range from 69 to 86 across 10 studies (Bar-On, 1997).

3. Competency Model

One of the most comprehensive models of emotional intelligence is the Competency model by Goleman. According to Goleman (1995) emotional intelligence consists of "abilities such as being able to motivate oneself and persist in the face of frustrations: to control impulse and delay gratification: to regulate one's moods and keep distress from swamping the ability to think; to empathize, and to hope". Goleman (1998) defined emotional intelligence in terms of self-awareness, self-confidence, self-control, commitment and integrity, and a person's ability to communicate, influence, initiate change and accept change. Goleman's model is specific to the domain of work performance. According to Goleman (1998) emotional intelligence is a combination of competencies, which contribute to a person's ability to manage and monitor his/her own emotions, to correctly gauge the emotional state of self and others and to influence opinions.

Based on extensive research, Goleman (1995, 1998) proposed five dimensions of emotional intelligence consisting of 25 competencies. The three dimensions of self-awareness, self-regulation, and self-motivation are personal competencies whereas empathy and social skills are social competencies.

- Self-awareness:
  - a. emotional self-awareness,
  - b. accurate self-assessment, and
  - c. self-confidence.
- Self-regulation:
  - a. self-control,
  - b. trustworthiness,
  - c. conscientiousness,
  - d. adaptability, and
  - e. innovation.
- Self-motivation:

a. achievement drive,

b. commitment,

c. initiative, and

d. optimism.

- Empathy:

  a. understanding of others,

  b. developing others,

  c. service orientation,

  d. leveraging diversity and

  e. political awareness, and

- Social skills:

  a influence

  b. communication,

  c. conflict management,

  d. leadership,

  e. change catalyst,

  f. building bond,

  g. collaboration and cooperation, and

  h. team capabilities.

Later another model evolved, which reflects the analysis wherein the 25 competencies were collapsed into 20 and five domains into four (Boyatzis, Goleman, & Rhee, 2000).

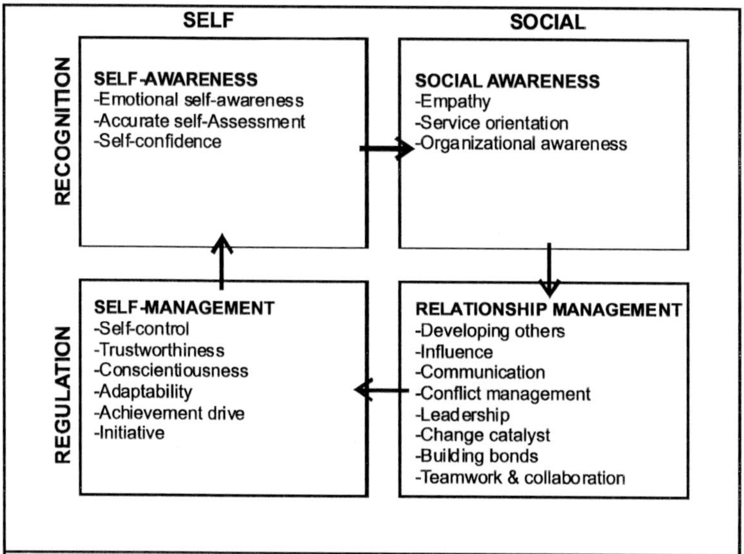

Figure 3.3 – Competency Model of Emotional Intelligence

(Adapted from Boyatzis, Goleman, & Rhee, 2000).

In the revised model, the first component of emotional intelligence is emotional self-awareness i.e. knowing what one feels, and awareness of one's internal states, preferences, and resources. The second component, emotional self-management is the ability to manage one's internal states and resources. Social awareness refers to awareness of others' feelings, needs, and concerns. The last component, relationship management focusses on our ability to attune ourselves or to influence the emotion of another person.

Based on the work of Boyatzis and Goleman, the Emotional Competence Inventory (ECI) is a 360 degree instrument that generates ratings on a series of behavioural indicators of emotional intelligence. The ECI encompasses 20 competencies, organized into four Clusters: Self-Awareness, Social-Awareness, Self-Management, and Social Skills (Boyatzis et al., 2000). The ECI has high levels of internal consistency. Emotional Competence Inventory (ECI) Version 2 consists of only 18 competencies grouped into four dimensions: Self-Awareness, Self-Management, Social Awareness and Social Skills.

Another measure is the EQ Map (Orioli, Jones, & Trocki, 1999). It helps to discover current environment awareness, competencies, values/beliefs and life outcomes that make up a person's emotional intelligence. It is made up of 20 scales measuring emotional intelligence and its effects on one's life both personally and professionally.

Saarni (1999) identified emotional competence as the ability to understand, manage, and express the social and emotional aspects of one's life in ways that enable the successful management of life. It includes self-awareness, emotional regulation, working cooperatively, and caring about oneself and others. He proposed eight skills of an emotionally intelligent person:

(a) being aware of one's own sometimes complex emotional state,

(b) being able to discern others' emotional states,

(c) being able to state and communicate one's emotions,

(d) being able to feel with and for others,

(e) being able to understand that people do not always show emotions accurately,

(f) being able to cope with difficult emotional communication when relating to others,

(g) being aware of emotional communications in interpersonal relationships, and

(h) being aware that one is in charge of one's feelings and may choose one's emotional response in a given situation.

4. The Trait Emotional Intelligence Model

Petrides et al.(2000, 2004 & 2007) distinguished between the ability based model and a trait based model of emotional intelligence. They defined trait emotional intelligence or trait emotional self-efficacy as an individual's self-perceptions of their emotional abilities and the belief that one can achieve desired outcomes in the emotional realm. According to Suveg & Zeman (2004), emotional self-efficacy is a component of emotional regulation.

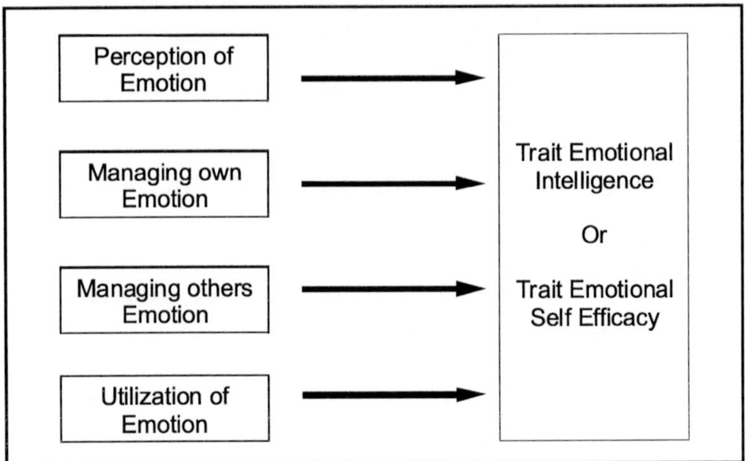

Figure 3.4 – Petrides et al. Model of Trait Emotional Intelligence

Saarni (2000) hypothesized that emotional self-efficacy is a key facilitator of subjective well- being in youth. Emotional self-efficacy is especially predictive of psychopathology particularly anxiety (Suveg & Zeman, 2004).

The Assessing Emotions Scale (Schutte et al., 1998) consists of 33 items responded to on a five point Likert type scale. It measures the original Salovey and Mayer's (1990) model of emotional intelligence. Factor analysis of the initial 62 items resulted in the single-factor, 33-item scale, which has good internal consistency and test-retest reliability.

The Trait Emotional Intelligence Questionnaire (TEIQue) provides an operationalization for Petrides and colleagues' model of emotional intelligence. The test encompasses 15 subscales organized under four factors: Well-Being, Self-

Control, Emotionality, and Sociability. Other scales, which measure emotional intelligence in the trait domain are: Trait Meta Mood Scale (TMMS; Salovey, Mayer, Goldman, Turvey, & Palfai, 1995); Dulewicz and Higgs Emotional Intelligence Questionnaire (Dulewicz & Higgs, 2001) etc.

□□□

4

Indian View of Emotional Intelligence

Emotional intelligence is quite a new concept with a history of research of around 25 years. In this duration many researches have been conducted on this topic. However, most of these researches have taken place in the West. Research on emotional intelligence has been happening for more than a decade now in India as well. The concept of emotional intelligence can be found in ancient Indian texts. In the Bhagavad Gita, Sri Krishna told Arjuna, "You must be free from the pairs of opposites, poise your mind in tranquillity". Likewise, many ancient Indian texts discuss the concept of emotional balance, which depicts the concept of emotional intelligence. According to Pragadeeswaran and Panchanatham (2003) "Equilibrium of emotional functions of mind with thought functions is called EQ or emotional intelligence or equanimity."

Emotional intelligence in the Indian context cannot be viewed as a homogenous trait, or a mental ability devoid of social concerns like respecting elders, concern for others, fulfilling one's duties. These along with moral values of Ahimsa (non-violence), kindness, benevolence, provide the very basis for emotional expression and responsivity and how an individual deals with emotional, socio-cultural situations. These culture specific ways of behaving, therefore, are basic to the notion of emotional intelligence. It is due to these reasons that individuals approach emotions differently-across cultures. (Sibia, Srivastva & Mishra, 2005)

Sibia, Srivastva and Mishra (2005) have proposed that the concept of emotional intelligence is embedded in its highly valued cultural practices. They developed an interview schedule to examine the perceptions of parents, teachers and children regarding emotional intelligence characteristics. They have proposed a culturally appropriate model of emotional intelligence keeping in mind the distinctive features of the Indian culture. It includes the following components of emotional intelligence – social sensitivity, time orientation, pro social values, action tendencies and affective states.

In India as in the West, the assessment of emotional intelligence has emerged rather slowly. While some researchers have developed psychometric assessment tools, others have tried to undertake qualitative methods for understanding emotional intelligence. Thingujam and Ram (2000) made an attempt at Indian adaptation of the Emotional Intelligence Scale (Schutte et al. 1998) but no item modification was made. Indian norms for males and females were also developed separately. The internal consistency of the tool was estimated at 0.89. They made a classification of the individual status on emotional intelligence ranging from below average to very superior, which is based on general intelligence classification. Women significantly scored higher than men. As a part of the convergent validity studies they also reported that emotional intelligence was correlated strongly and positively with coping with stress, moderately and negatively with trait-anxiety, and slightly and positively with belief in social relation (Thingujam & Ram, 1999).

Singh (2001) authored the book *Emotional intelligence at work: A professional guide*. Singh and Chadha (2001) developed the Emotional Quotient Test for the Indian population. This test was designed to measure emotional sensitivity, emotional maturity and emotional competency. The test contains fifteen situations measuring different emotional responses and their blends. Shanwal (2004) adapted the Emotional Intelligence Test (Mayer &Salovey, 2000) by modifying the items to suit the Indian context. Bhattacharya, Dutta and Mandal (2004) conducted a study to examine the factor structure of emotional intelligence in India. They adapted Emotional Intelligence Scale and found the following factors: appraisal of negative emotions; appraisal of positive emotions; interpersonal conflicts and flexibility; emotional facilitation and goal orientation.

Prakash and Pant (2004) evaluated the construct of emotional intelligence as assessed by the Multi Factor Emotional Intelligence Scale (MEIS). Performance on MEIS was correlated with theoretically relevant criterion measures. Results revealed low reliabilities with mixed relationship with various subtests of MEIS and no substantial gender difference among various emotional intelligence dimensions. The results suggest that the emotional intelligence construct is not a unique ability in the Indian sample as measured by MEIS. Singh (2004) initiated a study for developing and standardizing a measure of emotional intelligence following the Goleman (1998) model. Emotional intelligence was found to be positively correlated with organizational commitment, emotional expression and quality of life. Another set of work has employed qualitative methodology for understanding emotional intelligence. A measure of emotional intelligence was developed by Pandey and Tripathi (2003). It consisted of photographs and verbal descriptions involving different emotional situations following the work of Ekman, Friesen, and Ellsworth (1972). It had five sub areas:- Identification of emotion; Perception and recognition of emotion without probing; Perception and recognition of emotion with probing; Understanding emotional meanings and Emotion intensity rating.

The effect of emotional intelligence and self-efficacy on life satisfaction was studied by Anand (2013). The sample consisted of 120 undergraduate students studying in various colleges of University of Delhi, India. Results showed that emotional intelligence and self-efficacy are significant predictors of life satisfaction. Another study investigated the role of gratitude, emotional intelligence, and forgiveness in happiness (Anand, 2015). The sample consisted of 135 young adults living in Delhi and Chandigarh, India. Regression analysis showed that emotional intelligence and gratitude are significant predictors of happiness. These studies underline the importance of emotional intelligence in happiness and well-being.

Study by Anand (2015) aimed to enhance the level of emotional intelligence of undergraduate students. A two group pre-post design was used. The experimental group received training in emotional intelligence for two weeks whereas the control group did not receive any treatment. It was hypothesized that emotional intelligence of the experimental group will be enhanced after training. Mixed ANOVA results showed a significant difference between the experimental and control groups after training. This showed that the training program was successful in enhancing emotional intelligence of the experimental group.

Research work on emotional intelligence is on the rise in India with more and more researchers taking interest in this topic.

□□□

5

Importance of Emotional Intelligence

Emotional intelligence has emerged as a very popular and useful construct in Psychology. It has found applications in industrial and organizational psychology, developmental, clinical, counselling, and social psychology among many others.

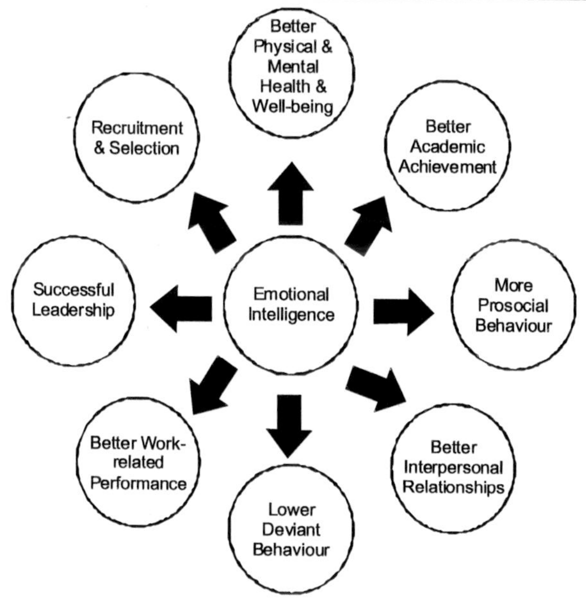

Figure 5.1 – Importance of Emotional Intelligence

Emotional Intelligence and Academic Performance

Emotional intelligence has been found to be positively related to academic performance. Students high in emotional intelligence have been found to have higher academic achievement. Emotional intelligence correlates with grades about r = .20 to .25 among college students (Ashkanasy & Dasborough, 2003; Brackett & Mayer, 2003). The positive relationship between emotional intelligence and academic achievement could be due to the fact that students high in emotional intelligence have better impulse control and can manage stress and anxiety in a better way thereby facilitating their study work.

Bar-On (1997) reported that emotional quotient was a strong predictor of academic progress among highly successful versus less successful students. Downey, Mountstephen, Lloyd, Hansen, and Stough, (2008) examined the relationship between emotional intelligence and scholastic achievement and found that higher academic achievement was associated with higher emotional intelligence.

Emotional Intelligence as Predictor of Deviant Behavior

Deviant behavior can occur in many forms like violence, bullying, substance abuse etc. The causes of such problems largely lie in lack of empathy, poor impulse control, poor ability to manage emotions and poor social competence. Due to these the individual may suffer from low self-esteem, which might further aggravate the situation and make them more prone to anti-social and deviant behaviors.

When a person has low empathy and compassion they lack the ability to understand the emotions of others. Individuals with low emotional intelligence may also misinterpret ambiguous cues in the environment as offensive or threatening and may react to such situations with violent behavior. Hence, low emotional intelligence is one of the main causes of anti-social or deviant behavior.

In many studies emotional intelligence has been found to be negatively related to deviant and problem behavior. Studies suggest that lower emotional intelligence is related to involvement in self-destructive behaviours such as deviant behaviour and cigarette smoking (Brackett & Mayer, 2003). Emotional intelligence varies inversely with bullying, violence, tobacco use, and drug problems (Trinidad & Johnson, 2002). Swift (2002) reported a negative relationship between perceiving emotions and aggression. Lower emotional intelligence has been associated with higher reported use of drugs and alcohol, more deviant behavior, and owning large numbers of self-help books (Mayer, Caruso, & Salovey, 1999; Trinidad & Johnson, 2002).

Emotional Intelligence and Prosocial Behavior

Empathy is the cornerstone of emotional intelligence. It is through empathy that one can be aware of others' emotions and needs. Individuals higher in emotional intelligence have better social awareness. Due to better understanding of others' needs, individuals with high emotional intelligence perform more prosocial behaviour. This also helps them in developing and maintaining relationships.

Emotional Intelligence and Interpersonal Relationships

Emotional intelligence plays a very important role in interpersonal relationships. A very important element in the success of any relationship is communication skills. Individuals with high emotional intelligence have been found to be better at communication. Another important component of successful relationships is conflict management. If a person has high emotional intelligence they are better at handling conflicts. With such characteristics individuals high in emotional intelligence can develop and maintain relationships in a better way.

Many studies provide evidence for this. Managing emotion was found to correlate positively with the quality of interaction with friends (Lopes, Salovey, & Straus, 2003). Pupils high on trait emotional intelligence were found to be higher on prosocial behavior and lower on antisocial factor. Relationships play a crucial role in one's physical and mental well-being. A meta-analysis of results based on 1188 participants found an overall association of r=.23 between higher emotional intelligence and greater romantic relationship satisfaction (Malouff, Schutte & Thorsteinsson, 2012). Self-reported parental warmth and secure attachment style also positively correlated with emotional intelligence (Mayer, Caruso, & Salovey, 1999).

Emotional Intelligence and Stress Management

Individuals experience greater stress in today's world due to increasing competition and pressures. One of the major causes of stress these days is abusive and unsatisfying relationships. Since individuals with higher emotional intelligence are able to have better relationships, therefore stress experienced due to relationships is less in such individuals. The various components of emotional intelligence can help us in understanding this relationship between emotional intelligence and stress management. Through self-awareness one can understand whether one is feeling stressed, as well as the causes of stress. Whether the stressor is any person or object in the environment or merely one's self-talk. Emotional intelligence helps in understanding the causes of stress. It also helps in understanding that stress can be managed. Individuals high in emotional intelligence are aware of various ways of managing stress such as self-management or emotional regulation. Emotional intelligence helps in handling stress better. Gohm, Corser, and Dalsky (2005) found that emotional intelligence was positively related to stress management among college students who either closely attended to their emotion or regularly distanced from and intellectualized their feelings.

Emotional Intelligence and Work-related Performance

Emotional intelligence has been found to play a positive role in one's performance at work. Through self-awareness one is aware of their strengths and weaknesses and can therefore work accordingly. Employees can work on capitalizing their strengths and overcoming their deficiencies. Through self-regulation they can manage stress and anxiety better. High emotional intelligence helps in developing and maintaining relationships at the workplace. It also helps in developing higher social awareness. All these factors contribute to better performance.

According to Goleman (1998) competency research in over two hundred companies and organizations worldwide has shown that about one-third of the difference in efficiency is due to technical skill and cognitive ability while two-thirds is due to emotional competence. Emotional intelligence is related to more profits in a consulting firm (Boyatzis, 1999). It has been reported that for jobs of all kinds, emotional competencies are twice as important as technical skills and purely cognitive abilities combined (Goleman, 1998).

Emotional intelligence has been found to distinguish between star performers and average performers (Spencer, 1997). Emotional intelligence was also found to lead to more policy sales (Hay/McBer Research Innovation Group, 1997); reduction in lost time accidents and formal grievances and increase in productivity (Pesuric & Byham, 1996). Emotional intelligence was related to success as a store manager in a retail chain (Lusch & Serpkeuci, 1990), and increased productivity in insurance companies (Seligman, 1990). At L'Oreal, sales agents selected on the basis of certain emotional competencies significantly outsold salespeople selected using the company's old selection procedure (Spencer & Spencer, 1993; Spencer, McClelland, & Kelner, 1997).

A meta-analysis of emotional intelligence and work performance (Joseph & Newman, 2010) reported an association between higher ability emotional intelligence and better performance. Another meta-analysis of 43 effect sizes for the relationships between emotional intelligence and work performance (O'Boyle, Humphrey, Pollack, Hawver, & Story, 2011) found associations of r=.24 for ability measures of emotional intelligence and .30 for self-report and peer report based trait measures of emotional intelligence.

Emotional Intelligence and Leadership

According to Goleman (1998), emotional intelligence distinguishes between a truly great leader and a mediocre one. As one climbs up the organizational ladder, the skill of emotional intelligence becomes more crucial. Numerous studies have shown the relationship between emotional intelligence and leadership success.

Barling, Slater, and Kelloway (2000) studied the relationship between transformational leadership and emotional intelligence and suggested that emotional intelligence predisposes leaders to use behaviours that are transformational. He found that emotional intelligence was positively related to three components of transformational leadership: Idealized Influence, Inspirational Motivation, and Individualized Consideration and Contingent Reward (Transactional Leadership).

Srivastava and Bharamanaikar (2004) found that emotional intelligence significantly correlated with transformational leadership and success. Bhalla and Nauriyal (2004) analyzed the role of emotional intelligence in managing organizations and in leadership development process. They concluded that emotional intelligence has found increased acceptance as a factor that is potentially useful in understanding and predicting individual performance at work. They also highlighted the importance of emotional intelligence in today's fast changing corporate environment. Emotional intelligence is related to effective managerial skills (Slaski & Cartwright, 2002); effective managerial behaviour (Sivanathan & Fekken, 2002) and leadership excellence (Ruderman, Hannum, Leslie, & Steed, 2001).

67% of success of a leader is determined by emotional social intelligence (Bar-On, Handley, & Fund, 2005) and 80% of exceptional performance can be accounted on the basis of emotional intelligence (Goleman, 1998). Singh (2004) found that emotional intelligence was positively correlated with organizational commitment, emotional expression and quality of life.

The US Air Force found that the most successful recruiters scored significantly higher in the emotional intelligence competencies of assertiveness, empathy, happiness, and emotional self-awareness. An analysis of more than 300 top-level executives from fifteen global companies showed that six emotional competencies distinguished stars from the average: influence, team leadership, organizational awareness, self-confidence, achievement drive, and leadership (Spencer, 1997).

Emotionally intelligent leadership helps in creating a healthy work environment that encourages employees to give their best. This leads to improved business performance. In a study of CEOs in U.S. insurance companies, companies in which CEOs exhibited more emotional intelligence competencies showed better financial results as measured by both profit and growth (Williams, 1994).

A similar relationship between emotional intelligence strengths in a leader and business results was found by McClelland (1998). The divisions of the leaders with a critical mass of emotional intelligence strengths outperformed yearly revenue targets by a margin of 15 to 20 percent. The divisions of the leaders weak in emotional intelligence competencies underperformed by about the same margin (Goleman, 1998).

Heads of forty-two schools in the United Kingdom were studied and it was found that leadership style increased students' academic achievement by directly affecting school climate. When the school head had a flexible leadership style and high emotional intelligence, teachers' attitudes were more positive and students' grades higher. However, when the leader relied on fewer emotional intelligence competencies, teachers were more demoralized and students underperformed academically (Hay/McBer, 2000).

Emotional Intelligence and Recruitment and Selection

Recruitment and selection are very important human resource activities in organizations. A lot of effort goes into selecting the right person for the right job. Since many studies have shown that individuals high in emotional intelligence have better workplace productivity, lesser absenteeism, fewer accidents etc., it becomes crucial that organizations use emotional intelligence as a criterion to recruit candidates.

Hay MacBer research innovation group (1997) differentiated between outstanding and typical performers on the basis of a selection process based on emotional intelligence. The US Air Force found that the most successful recruiters scored significantly higher in the emotional intelligence competencies, which resulted in a saving of $3 million annually (Handley, 1997).

In research at Met Life, Seligman and his colleagues (1990) found that new salesmen who were optimists sold 37 percent more insurance in their first two years than did pessimists. The group, which scored high on optimism, outsold the pessimists by 21 percent in their first year and 57 percent in the second. They even outsold the average agent by 27 percent.

Emotional Intelligence and Physical and Mental Health and Well-being

Emotional intelligence plays a crucial role in mental and physical health and well-being. Since emotional intelligence is significantly positively correlated to positive outcomes like satisfying relationships, higher workplace productivity, better stress management, and more involvement in prosocial behaviour, all these have a spill over effect on one's health and well-being. An important benchmark of emotional intelligence is healthier and satisfying relationships. Many studies have shown the crucial link between social support and better health. Individuals with high EQ are more likely to have positive social interactions, which results in better health and well-being.

In terms of the relationship between emotional intelligence and health behaviours, it would be useful to see whether individuals high in emotional intelligence are healthier than those who have lower emotional intelligence, and vice versa. A study by Bar-On (2012) found that people who are more emotionally intelligent feel healthier than those who are less emotionally intelligent. Nearly 25% of self-perceived physical health was found to be influenced by one's level of emotional intelligence. Self-regard was found to be the strongest predictor of health. Other strong emotional intelligence predictors of physical health were self-actualisation, stress tolerance, optimism and happiness (Bar-On, 2012).

Another important component of emotional intelligence is self-control. This plays a crucial role in physical health in terms of eating a healthy diet, exercising, not getting involved in substance abuse etc. Also self-control involves not letting anxieties, worries, and stresses to overwhelm oneself and effectively managing one's emotions. All this has positive effects on one's health and well-being.

Meta-analyses (Martins, Ramalho, & Morin, 2010; Schutte, Malouff, Thorsteinsson, Bhullar, & Rooke, 2007) have shown the relationship between higher emotional intelligence and better mental and physical health across numerous studies. This meta-analysis reported significant relationships between emotional intelligence and mental health, r=.36, psychosomatic health, r=.33, and physical health, r=.27. Studies by (Anand, 2013, 2015) have found emotional intelligence to be a significant predictor of happiness. These studies underline the importance of emotional intelligence in happiness and well-being.

To conclude, emotional intelligence has been linked to many positive outcomes like higher academic achievement, more workplace productivity, better leadership, appropriate recruitment and selection, higher social support, and better physical and mental health and well-being. Hence, emotional intelligence has proved to be a very important area of research and application in all domains of life.

□□□

6

Emotional Intelligence as a Learnable Competency

Often there is a debate as to whether people are born with certain qualities or characteristics or do these develop over the course of one's life. Likewise goes the debate for emotional intelligence. It is debated whether people are born with a certain level of emotional intelligence or do these emotional intelligence competencies develop through out their life as a result of life experiences. Evidence has been found for both.

Given the importance of emotional intelligence in various domains of life it is a desirable competency to have. Emotional intelligence assumes critical importance in today's world as it is facing grave challenges in the form of violence, stress, depression, unsatisfying relationships and unhappiness. Most of these problems are rooted in emotional mismanagement. The good news isthat emotional intelligence can be learnt! Individuals and organizations throughout the world have started making efforts to incorporate emotional intelligence in their work and life. Teachers, parents, administrators, politicians etc. should be trained in emotional intelligence. The best way to bring about a significant change is to start early. Hence, children should be trained in emotional intelligence from the very beginning. Parents and teachers need to inculcate emotional intelligence in children. Countries throughout the world should incorporate the competencies of emotional intelligence in the curriculum. If children are trained from the very beginning in understanding and managing emotions they will grow up to be responsible citizens who not only are emotionally healthy themselves but also contribute to the betterment of the society.

Emotional intelligence evolves in the neurotransmitters of the brain's limbic system, which plays an important role in our feelings, impulses, and drives. The limbic system learns through motivation, practice, and feedback. In contrast, the neocortex is responsible for concepts and logic and learns technical and cognitive abilities very quickly. The evidence that emotional intelligence can be learnt started coming from the following early researches: McClelland and colleagues' research on developing achievement and power motivation; Kolb and his colleagues' work on self-directed behavioural change; and research on competency development at the Weather head School of Management at Case Western Reserve University.

Even though genes play an important role in emotional intelligence, psychological research shows the important role of nurture too. Hence, emotional intelligence is not a fixed characteristic. It can be developed. Emotional intelligence can be learnt at any age but it needs practice and motivation. Findings suggest that emotional intelligence increases with age, i.e. older people display higher levels of emotional intelligence than do younger people (Bar-On and Parker, 2000; Mayer, Salovey, Caruso, Sitarenios, 2001; Van Rooy, Viswesvaran, & Pluta, 2005).

So all problems related to lack of emotional self-awareness, low self-confidence, low empathy and poor relationships should not be taken as determined by one's destiny and hence fixed. These problems can be overcome by developing the competency of emotional intelligence.

Effects of Emotional Intelligence Intervention Programs

Most of the work done on emotional intelligence till date consists of correlational studies. Very few studies have been undertaken where interventions on emotional intelligence were designed and administered and their effects being studied. These studies according to their domains are discussed below.

Organizations

A study conducted by Slaski and Cartwright (2002, 2003) consisted of 120 retail managers from one retail chain who were divided into a control group of 60 and a training group of 60 who were provided with an intervention. The results indicated that the emotional intelligence scores of the training group increased significantly from pre to post training.

Another study focused on the effectiveness of a staff training directed at emotional intelligence and interactions between staff and clients (Zijlmans, Embregts, Gerits, Bosman, & Derksen, 2011). Participants were 214 support staff working within residential settings for individuals with ID and challenging behaviour. The experimental group consisted of 76 staff members, 138 staff members participated in two different control groups. A pre-test, post-test, follow-up control group design was used. Emotional intelligence of the experimental group changed significantly more than that of the two control groups.

Groves, McEnrue, and Shen (2008) gave employees an 11 week training program on emotional intelligence. They found the training group as having higher emotional intelligence after training than employees in a non-random assignment comparison group. Kirk, Schutte and Hine (2011) provided emotional self-efficacy training to employees randomly assigned to the intervention condition. After the training, employees scored higher on emotional intelligence, emotional self-efficacy and workplace civility than employees in the control condition.

Education

Study by Anand (2015) aimed to enhance the level of emotional intelligence of undergraduate students. A two group pre-post design was used. The experimental group received training in emotional intelligence for two weeks whereas the control group did not receive any treatment. It was hypothesized that emotional intelligence of the experimental group will be enhanced after training. Mixed ANOVA results showed a significant difference between the experimental and control groups after training. This showed that the training program was successful in enhancing emotional intelligence of the experimental group.

Schutte and Malouff (2002) provided beginning university students with information and skills training related to emotional intelligence. The students who received emotional intelligence training scored significantly higher on emotional intelligence at the end of the term and were more likely to complete their first year of university than control students with no intervention. In a study with MBA students, Reuben, Sapienza, and Zingales (2009) found that those randomly assigned to a 16-hour course designed to teach the abilities described by the ability model, scored significantly higher on a performance test of emotional intelligence than those assigned to aplacebo control group.

In their meta-analysis of 213 Social and Emotional Learning (SEL) intervention studies, Durlak, Weissberg, Dymnicki, Taylor and Schellinger (2011) found significant mean effects for SEL interventions in improved social emotional skills (at d = .57) and positive social behaviour (d = .24), fewer conduct problems (d =.24) and lesser emotional distress (d = .24), and better academic performance (d = .27).

A study was done, which followed a quasi-experimental pre-post design on two groups of first year university students from two universities in north Jordan (Jdaitawi,

Ishak, Tamneh, Gharaibeh, Rababah, 2011). The experimental group received ten days on an hour to an hour and half sessions of emotional intelligence training, while the control group was only given pre-post questionnaires. Results showed that the training program was effective in significantly raising the level of emotional intelligence.

Nelis et al. (2011) found increased emotional intelligence in participants in the emotional intelligence intervention group as compared to the control group. Review of emotional intelligence training programs with school children indicates beneficial effects for school related as well as interpersonal relations (Brackett & Katulak, 2006).

In a study that aimed to find out the relationship between emotion regulation and job satisfaction and burnout among secondary school teachers, it was found that emotion regulation in teachers is associated with positive affect, job satisfaction, feelings of personal accomplishment, and support from principals (Brackett, Palomera, Mojsa-Kaja, Reyes, & Salovey, 2010).

Physical and Mental Health and Well-being

In a large-scale study, adolescents who participated in 24 emotional intelligence training sessions over two years, had higher emotional intelligence and they also experienced less depression and social stress compared to adolescents in a non-random assignment control group (Ruiz-Aranda et al., 2012).

A study on 941 male conscripts into the Israeli Defence Forces (IDF), with an average age of 18 years was conducted. It indicated that one's ability (a) to manage emotions and cope with stress, (b) be flexible and adaptable, (c) solve personal and interpersonal problems, (d) achieve personal goals designed to actualise their potential as well as the ability to be (e) optimistic and (f) content with themselves, others and life in general significantly differentiated between less healthy and healthier individuals (Bar-On, 2012).

Bar-On (2012) examined the impact of emotional intelligence on health in a sample of coronary heart disease patients who suffered myocardial infarction (MI). The results indicate that the MI patients exhibited significant deficiencies in their stress tolerance, problem solving, flexibility and happiness when compared with the control group.

Another study (Bar-On, 2012) examined differences in emotional intelligence between 35 cancer survivors and a matched non-clinical sample. This study was conducted in the Paediatric Oncology Department at Rambam Hospital in Israel. The cancer survivors' level of optimism was found to be significantly higher than the non-clinical subjects. Multiple regression analysis showed emotional intelligence to be a significant predictor of health behaviours contributing to around 20% of the variance. Results of the study are in congruence with existing studies, which show high emotional intelligence and optimism to be positively related to good health behaviours and better health (eg. Bar-On, 2012; Scheier & Carver, 1985; Scheier, et al., 1989).

Importance of Developing Emotional Intelligence

Looking at the relationship between emotional competence in individuals, group and community well-being and their success it is really important that such skills are taught. It is very important for young people to develop these competencies. However, the current education system does not teach the skills to deal with challenges prevailing in the contemporary society. Education must not only serve as a step towards gaining employment but the total personality development of the individual.

There are many school based programs that undertake imparting the basics of emotional intelligence programs that deal with social and emotional learning. Innovative schools and educational organizations have now started integrating emotional intelligence into their educational programs through social and emotional learning.

However, given the importance of such skills, the efforts made in this direction are not sufficient. The Social and Emotional Learning (SEL) course exists for early school years but not for higher education. The importance of emotional intelligence at the workplace has also been underlined. Therefore, it is important that college students are also taught these crucial skills as adolescence and late adolescence are challenging stages of life characterized by various stresses.

The Collaborative for Social and Emotional Learning (CASEL) was founded in 1994 and is a leading organization, which aims at identifying the best educational practices to maximize healthy social and emotional development of children, academic achievement, ethical behaviour, and citizenship.

Another study found that one year after schools that used RULER (Recognizing emotions in self and others, Understanding the causes and consequences of emotions, Labelling emotions accurately, Expressing emotions appropriately, Regulating emotions effectively) as compared with those that used the standard curriculum were rated as having higher degree of warmth between students and teachers, less bullying among students, and teachers were found to focus more on the interests and motivations of the students (Rivers, Brackett, Reyes, Elbertson, & Salovey, 2013).

When teachers develop their own emotional intelligence skills, they may feel motivated and happy to connect to each other. In such an environment students feel safe in their relationships, are motivated to learn, and achieve. Not only teachers but administrators too must develop social and emotional skills. They can help in developing schools and communities that support the development of caring, compassionate, motivated and successful individuals, friends, family members, and engaged citizens of the world (Patti, Senge, Madrazo, & Stern, 2015).

□□□

7

Controversies and Criticisms Surrounding Emotional Intelligence

Even though emotional intelligence has grown as an area of research and practice immensely, it is not free from controversies and criticisms. Here are some of the issues related to emotional intelligence.

Intelligence Quotient (IQ) vs Emotional Quotient (EQ)

Traditionally the concept of intelligence described how well a person's cognitive processes work. However, despite being a popular concept for a long time, the concept of intelligence has received a lot of criticism. One of the primary reasons is its failure to explain real life experiences (Sternberg, Wagner, Williams, & Hovarth, 1995). According to Gardner (1993), a large share one's ultimate niche in society is determined by non-IQ factors.

A variety of studies have shown that the dichotomy between cognition and affect is redundant. Emotions contribute to thought, and are related to one's personality.

According to Saarni (2001) emotional intelligence refers to a thinker with a heart who applies his/her mental abilities to perceiving, understanding and managing social relations. "The concept of emotional intelligence is primarily focused on the complex and potentially intelligent tapestry of emotional reasoning in everyday life" (Mayer & Salovey, 1997).

According to Spinoza (1677/1989), both emotion and the intellect together contribute to the ultimate cognitive tool. He talked about three levels of cognition (Knowledge) that is emotional cognition, intellectual cognition and intuition. Ellis (1962) pointed out that human emotion and thinking are not separate processes, but they significantly overlap. Mowrer (1960) said that "the emotions are of quite extraordinary importance in the total economy of living organisms and do not deserve being put into opposition with intelligence."

The concept of emotional intelligence shows that to understand and appreciate intelligence in totality one needs to attend to the domains of personality, emotions and motivation (Mayer & Salovey, 1997; Mayer, Caruso &Salovey, 1999). Goleman (1995, 1998, & 2001) in his model of emotional intelligence has also emphasized upon the balanced usage of emotion and intelligence. Salovey and Mayer (1997) asserted that emotions, it seems, themselves represent a higher order of intelligence. Mahoney (1991) also stated that cognitive constructivists view feeling, knowing and acting as inseparable experiences of adaptation and development of human beings. Similarly, Goleman (2000) also asserted that intelligence and emotional intelligence should not be regarded as competencies with an opposite direction.

In the dance of feeling and thought, the emotional faculty guides moment to moment decisions working hand in hand with the rational mind (Damasio, 1994). How a person does in life is not determined just by IQ but EQ also.

The media has created an impression that high EQ individuals might compensate for low IQ and help those with below average IQ, but high emotional intelligence can flourish. This has led to the belief that IQ has little value in life. Despite this controversy, the emotional intelligence paradigm has helped in bringing about a more balanced view of the role of cognition and emotion in determining life outcomes. However, more research is needed to validate these claims.

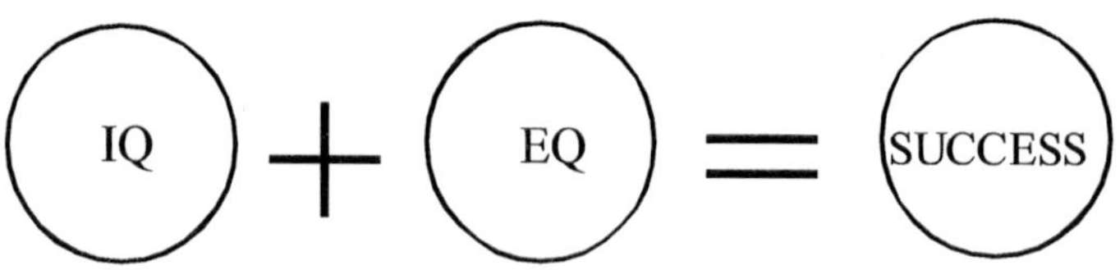

Figure 7.1 – Importance of both IQ and EQ in Success

Multiple theories of emotional intelligence

There are several theories/models of emotional intelligence (eg. Bar-On, 2000, Goleman, 1995, 1998, Mayer

&Salovey, 1997). However, the existence of these multiple theories creates confusion regarding the concept of emotional intelligence as each of them defines emotional intelligence from a different perspective. Since the construct of emotional intelligence is quite complex hence it is difficult to have a single theoretical model for explaining it.

Problems in Measurement

Historically emotions have been seen as irrational. Due to this notion many critics believe that it is difficult to correctly assess emotions or emotional intelligence.

Non-clarity of the Construct

The MEIS and MSCEIT have shown to be moderately correlated with IQ as their authors view that all forms of intelligence should show some correlation to be classified as an intelligence. The Bar-On EQ-i and other trait based theories of emotional intelligence show a high degree of overlap with traditional measures of personality (Bar-On, 1997; Schutte et al., 1998).

Critics feel that the concept of intelligence is being stretched too far from its original focus on mental ability. Some of the problems with the current models of emotional intelligence are as follows: the problem with the ability model is that it regards emotional intelligence as ability. Due to this emotional intelligence is considered as a quality, which is primarily fixed or cannot be changed. On the other hand, mixed models of emotional intelligence mix together qualities of emotional intelligence with other personality traits. This has led to confusion regarding the very concept of emotional intelligence and various questions regarding its validity as a new construct. Also the most popular model of emotional intelligence, the Goleman's model is a mixed model and is limited to the context of the workplace.

Davies, Stankov, and Roberts (1998) concluded that there was nothing empirically new in the idea of emotional intelligence. This conclusion was based on a review of existing measures, which claimed to assess emotional intelligence at the point in time when they wrote that paper. However, most of those measures were new, and there was not yet much known about their psychometric properties. Emerging research suggests that emotional intelligence is in fact a distinct entity.

Researches have often been able to demonstrate the discriminant validity of trait based approach of emotional intelligence (Ciarrochi, Chan & Caputi, 2000; Schutte et al., 1998). Emotional intelligence has emerged as a unique construct that accounts for unique variance. There is also a need for a general model of emotional intelligence, which specifically describes characteristics related to understanding and managing emotions well. The next chapter contains a general model called the 3S model of emotional intelligence developed by the author.

□□□

8

The 3S Model of Emotional Intelligence (Anand, 2016)

Emotional intelligence has been approached in different ways by various researchers: some consider it as ability; some consider it a trait; while some look at it as a competency.

Salovey and Mayer's (1990), Mayer, Salovey, and Caruso's (2000) theory placed emotional intelligence within a model of intelligence wherein emotion and thought interact in meaningful and adaptive ways. Bar-On (1988) placed emotional intelligence in the context of personality theory and Goleman formulated emotional intelligence in terms of a theory of performance.

In the author's view emotional intelligence is a competency (Anand, 2016). This is because ability is more enduring, relatively fixed and hence cannot be developed. However, various researches (mentioned in chapter 6) show that emotional intelligence can be developed. Therefore, the author regards emotional intelligence as a competency. Hence, emotional intelligence has been defined by the author as follows:

"Emotional intelligence involves competencies related to understanding and managing one's own emotions, understanding others' emotions, developing and maintaining satisfying relationships with others and channelling one's emotional energy to create a positive self" (Anand, 2016).

The 3S model is based on years of research by the author on emotional intelligence. The model has been formulated on the basis of qualitative analysis of interviews with 243 adult participants (115 males, 128 females; young 140; old 103) in three cities of Delhi, Lucknow, and Chandigarh. Structured interviews were conducted with the participants. Following open ended questions were asked:

1. How can one understand and manage one's emotions effectively?
2. Why is it important to understand and manage one's emotions effectively?
3. What role do emotions play in our interpersonal relationships?
4. How can our emotions help us in becoming a better person?

Thematic analysis was carried out on the qualitative data obtained from the interviews, which led to various subthemes and three major themes: *Self-competence, Social competence, and Self-positive.* Hence, the thematic analysis of the interview data yielded the three main domains of emotional intelligence and the sub themes were the sub-dimensions of these domains.

The 3S model of emotional intelligence

Emotional intelligence according to 3S model can be broadly divided into three broad domains:

I. Self-competence

II. Social competence

III. Self-positive

I. Self-competence

The domain of Self-competence refers to the competencies present in the individual regarding their own self. This is a very broad domain and it consists of two components: Emotional Self-awareness, and emotional self-management. This domain involves all that is related to an individual-their awareness and understanding about their emotions, their own assessment about their strengths and weaknesses, as well as how well they manage their emotions. Let us now discuss the two components of Self-competence.

a. Emotional Self-awareness

Any step towards self-knowledge and self-improvement is only possible through self-awareness. 'Know thyself' goes the ancient Greek aphorism. Emotional Self-awareness is the first component of self-competence. It underlines the importance of recognizing one's own feelings.

Emotional Self-awareness refers to knowing what one feels and being aware of the emotions that one is experiencing. It involves being able to understand the physiological changes that occur due to experiencing a certain emotion. It also involves trying to understand the causes of one's emotional state. It is important to understand the effect of a certain emotional state on oneself and other domains of one's life. Only with this kind of understanding can one decide on how to behave in various situations.

Emotional Self-awareness also involves being able to label the emotion that one is experiencing. One of the important aspects of Emotional Self-awareness is understanding the link between how one feels and how it is related to one's thought processes and actions.

Emotional Self-awareness helps in understanding the nature of emotions and their intensity as well. Introspection is a very important part of Emotional Self-awareness. It refers to looking within oneself to gain self-knowledge.

Emotional Self-awareness also involves accurate self-assessment etc. having an accurate socio-emotional SWOC assessment. Socio-emotional SWOC involves having an accurate assessment of one's strengths, weaknesses, opportunities, and challenges. This is important so that we can manage ourselves and our relationships in a better way.

Individuals with accurate self-assessment competency are aware of their abilities and limitations, seek out feedback and learn from their mistakes, and know where they need to improve. On 360-degree competence assessments, average performers typically overestimate their strengths, whereas star performers rarely do; if anything, the stars tended to underestimate their abilities, an indicator of high internal standards (Goleman, 1998).

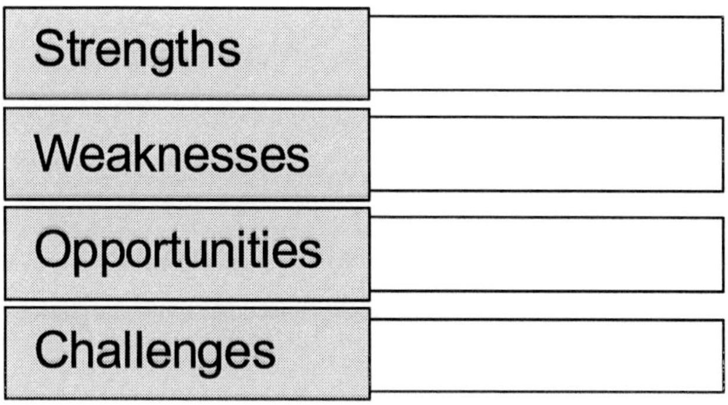

Fig. 8.1 - Socio-emotional SWOC

Important aspects of accurate self-assessment involve having an accurate view of oneself, knowing one's resources, learning from experience, being open to feedback, continuous learning and self-development, taking up tasks according to one's abilities etc. When we become aware of the areas in which we lack we can take necessary steps to overcome those limitations. When accurate self-assessment is lacking the individual may set unrealistic goals for himself/ herself. Doing this can increase their chances of failure. When failures and setbacks occur it can lead to frustrations in the individual. Accurate self-assessment helps in making one realize their potential, getting a realistic view of oneself, facilitates proper goal setting, and garnering motivation to achieve it. A very important component of accurate self-assessment is intentionally seeking feedback from others so as to develop a better understanding of oneself. Hence, Emotional Self-awareness is the cornerstone for emotional intelligence. It helps in developing awareness about one's emotions so it is the first step in the development of emotional intelligence.

Strategies for Developing Emotional Self-awareness

1. **Understanding concepts related to emotions:** In order to develop self-awareness an initial step would be to understand the concepts related to emotions.
2. **Knowing emotion related words:** Another step towards developing Emotional Self-awarenessis enhancing one's vocabulary of emotion related words. This will help in identifying and differentiating between various emotions.
3. **Experiencing the emotion:** A very important step towards developing Emotional Self-awareness is experiencing the emotion fully. This refers to understanding why a particular emotion has occurred as well as noticing the various physiological changes that occur during the experience of an emotion. One must observe one's emotions in various situations and how one reacts to the situation.
4. **Observing thoughts:** While experiencing any emotion the

individual must keenly observe their flow of thoughts and the reason behind these thoughts.

5. **Emotion journal:** A very useful step is to maintain a diary or journal to enter the various emotions and thoughts that one has experienced during the day. This will be an initial step towards planning for self-improvement.

6. **Observing the reactions of other people:** A very rich source of information for Emotional Self-awareness is observing the reactions of other people. They serve as a feedback for our emotional reactions and help in understanding our emotions.

7. **Introspection:** Introspection refers to looking within oneself. It is an important step as it helps in assessing oneself accurately.

8. **Learning from experience:** Our experience is an important teacher. It helps us in understanding our strengths and weaknesses and thereby making improvements in oneself.

9. **Valuing feedback from others:** Feedback from others in an important step in learning about oneself. Many times we are biased towards ourselves, which can be overcome by taking feedback from others. This will help in gaining realistic information about oneself.

10. **Reflecting upon feedback:** Next step is to analyse the feedback gained from others and incorporate that information for self-improvement.

11. **Capitalizing on one's strengths and working to overcome weaknesses:** After gathering information about oneself from introspection and feedback from others one can learn about their strengths. Once a person is able to know about their strengths, they can work towards maintaining and enhancing their strengths. When one is aware about one's weaknesses they can try to understand their causes. Then one can try to find ways to overcome weaknesses in the self.

12. **Preparing a SWOC list:** One must prepare a SWOC list where one's Strengths, Weaknesses, Opportunities, and Threats are noted down. This helps in accurate self-assessment.

13. **Writing a letter to oneself:** Another important way of developing self-awareness is to write a letter to one's past or future self. This will help in understanding one's goals, and motivations.

14. **Ask yourself:**

    a. What makes me unique?
    b. Who are my friends?
    c. What do I want to be?
    Follow up these questions with a "Why"?

b. Emotional Self-management

This is a crucial component of Self-competence, since managing one's emotions effectively is the cornerstone of one's well-being. Emotional Self-management means not being overwhelmed by failures and upcoming challenges.

Emotional Self-management involves exercising restraint over one's emotional expression. It also requires not letting disruptive emotions and impulses take over, and managing impulses and distressing emotions. Emotional Self-management incorporates the ability to think clearly under pressure and not let our emotions control us. However, this can only be achieved when we have gained proper understanding of our emotions. Emotional Self-management helps us in channelling our emotional energy for achievement of goals. It protects us from the dangers of our uncontrolled emotions and impulses. The ability to delay gratification plays a crucial role in academic and social success. The marshmallow experiment shows that the ability to resist impulse and have self-control is related to success.

Emotional Self-control involves the skill to remain calm, think clearly, stay focussed in the face of pressure and having control over one's mood swings. Through Emotional Self-control we have better and healthier relationships, which contribute to happiness. It also helps in proper adjustment. Among managers and executives, top performers are able to balance their drive and ambition with Emotional Self-control, harnessing their personal needs in the service of the organization's goals (Boyatzis, 1982).

General Strategies for Enhancing Emotional Self-management

- Using emotions in a positive way
- Reducing the intensity of emotion
- Trying to adopt a positive emotional state
- Anticipate the negative consequences of emotions
- Finding a safe outlet for venting
- Writing down about emotional experiences
- Seeking social support
- Stop blaming others
- Calming down

Three of the important domains in Emotional Self-management are anger management, anxiety management, and stress management. The strategies for each of these are as follows:

a. Anger Management Strategies

- Being aware of different words to describe anger
- Being aware of physiological changes in the body while experiencing anger.
- Being aware of the various thoughts while experiencing anger.
- Thinking of various ways how one reacts to the

situations that caused anger and then classifying them as productive or destructive.

- Identifying the situations that cause anger
- Understanding why it's important to manage anger
- Understanding the negative impact of venting out without thinking
- Understanding the effect on others if anger is not properly managed.
- Expressing anger in an assertive not aggressive manner
- Focussing on something positive
- Relaxation
- Cognitive restructuring: changing the way of thinking
- Changing the environment
- Using humour
- Taking time out
- Identifying possible solutions
- Calming down
- Talking to someone

b. Anxiety Management

- Being aware of different words used to describe anxiety

- Being aware of physiological changes in the body while experiencing anxiety.
- Being aware of the various thoughts while experiencing anxiety.
- Thinking of the various ways how one reacts to the situations that caused anxiety and then classify them as productive or destructive.
- Identifying the situations that cause anxiety
- Understanding why it is important to manage anxiety
- Understanding the ill-effects if anxiety is not properly managed.
- Taking time out
- Getting enough sleep
- Taking deep breaths
- Exercising daily
- Eating well-balanced meals
- Using humour
- Cognitive restructuring

c. **Stress Management**

- Being aware of different words used to describe stress
- Being aware of physiological changes in the body while experiencing stress.

- Being aware of the various thoughts while experiencing stress.
- Thinking of the various ways how one reacts to the situations that caused stress and then classify them as productive or destructive.
- Identifying the situations that cause stress
- Understanding why it's important to manage stress
- Understanding the ill-effects on one's physical and mental well-being, performance, and interpersonal relationships if stress is not properly managed.
- Understanding that some amount of stress is good for productive behaviour
- Yoga, meditation, and various forms of physical exercises, relaxation techniques
- Maintaining a healthy work-life balance
- Going out for a walk
- Listening to music
- Spending time with nature
- Time management
- Reframing problems
- Accepting things you can't change
- Distracting yourself
- Talking to someone
- Choosing an activity to engage in

- Engaging socially

II. Social Competence

The domain of Social competence involves the competencies in the individual that help them in interacting with others in their environment. So this is basically in relation to the social skills in an individual. This domain encompasses two main components: empathy, and developing and maintaining relationships.

a. Empathy

Empathy is considered to be the cornerstone of emotional intelligence. Empathy refers to an awareness of others' emotions, concerns, and needs. The empathic individual is able to read the emotions of others, and nonverbal cues such as facial expression, body language etc. An important requirement of empathy is self-awareness since we can only understand others' feelings when we are aware of our own feelings.

Empathy is quite beneficial. Due to empathy we can be sensitive to others. This is an important competency in all interpersonal relationships. Empathy leads to maintaining of long term relationships as one is able to understand the perspective and emotions of the other person. This also has implications in group settings. Since one is able to understand others, one is less likely to fall prey to stereotyping, prejudice, and discrimination. Empathy has implications for prosocial behaviour as well. Understanding the problems of others from their perspective leads to more helping behaviour. Empathic listening leads one to view the world as others view it. This leads to a better understanding of how others feel.

Through empathy one can become aware of others' emotions and therefore it helps in gaining social awareness. It refers to the ability to identify another person's needs. It involves the ability to understand the emotions and realities of one's social group. It helps in reading and understanding situations in one's environment. This awareness about others' emotions is essential as it helps in understanding their state of mind. It also helps in knowing if the other person is in distress or needs help.

Therefore, social awareness creates a sense of social responsibility in the person. Due to this the person feels responsible for others around them. This is a very important part of emotional intelligence as it incorporates a sense of responsibility. Individuals high in social responsibility perform behaviours that are beneficial for others. By being prosocial and understanding the needs of other people and groups they contribute to the betterment of the society.

Strategies to Develop Empathy

- Understanding that the perspective of others may differ from one's own perspective.
- Trying not to be judgmental towards others.
- Being accepting to the needs and emotions of others.

- Viewing a person's problem or situation from their perspective and not one's own.
- Valuing other people.
- Asking for forgiveness if one has transgressed.

b. Developing and Maintaining Relationships

The second component of Social competence is the competency of Developing and maintaining relationships. Developing and maintaining relationships depends on understanding the emotions of others, which refers to empathy. If one lacks empathy, one is not able to read the emotions of others, thereby behaving in ways that might hurt the other person. Relationships are built on trust and therefore having trust in others is an important part of Developing and maintaining relationships.

An emotionally intelligent person is adept at Developing and maintaining relationships. A very core aspect of Developing and maintaining relationships is how one expresses emotional information as well as how they receive it. It also involves being able to understand the emotional state of others. Individuals high in this competency know what not to speak or express so that the feelings of the other person are not hurt.

A very important aspect of Developing and maintaining relationships is communication. Individuals competent in communication are effective in the give-and-take of emotional information and prefer open communication.

Communication depends on managing one's own emotions and empathy; being attuned to others' emotional states and controlling the impulse to respond in ways that might cause harm to the relationship.

A very important aspect of Developing and maintaining relationships is Developing others. It means understanding the potential in others and then motivating them and providing them opportunities for growth and development. Developing others involves sensing the developmental needs of other people and helping them in realizing their potential. Competence in developing others is a hallmark of superior managers; among sales managers, for example, it typifies those at the top of the field (Spencer & Spencer, 1993).

As in most situations, in a conflict situation too our first reaction is emotional. The goal of emotional intelligence is to use increased awareness of emotions and effectively manage our interactions with others. People with high emotional intelligence are sensitive to the feelings of others. Jordan and Troth (2004) studied the relationship between emotional intelligence and preferred styles of conflict resolution and the results showed that emotionally intelligent individuals seek collaborative solutions in conflict situations. Some of these are as follows:

- Monitoring emotional triggers
- Reframing perceptions
- Reflective listening
- Choosing the right words in an argument.

Relationships involve a potential for conflict. Emotionally intelligent individuals are competent in managing conflicts. Such individuals have an open attitude towards managing conflicts. They are able to understand the perspective of the other person. Effective conflict management is a key quality of Developing and maintaining relationships

Conflict management involves identifying trouble as it emerges and taking steps to calm oneself and the people involved. Listening and empathizing are crucial skills for handling difficult people and situations, and having open discussion. Effective conflict management is crucial to long-terminter personal relationships. In a survey of retail buyers in department store chains, effectiveness at win-win negotiating was an accurate barometer of the health of the manufacturer-retailer relationship (Ganesan, 1993).

Strategies for Developing and Maintaining Relationships

- Understanding the importance of interpersonal relationships and social support in one's life.
- Valuing the needs, values, and emotions of other people.
- Not judging others by one's own standards
- Understanding the perspective of the other person
- Enhancing one's communication skills to achieve a healthy relationship with others

- In case of conflict, taking steps to resolve the conflict
- Identifying potential in others and helping them develop their talents and potential
- Understanding and respecting diversity
- Practicing Emotional Self-management so as not to hurt the feelings of others.
- Building trust in interpersonal relationships
- Giving direct and constructive feedback
- Expressing care and love for other people.
- Not giving mixed signals i.e. no incongruence between verbal and non-verbal communication.

III. SELF-POSITIVE

Self-positive is the third and final domain of emotional intelligence. It is the epitome of emotional intelligence. The first two domains of Self-competence and Social competence deal with all that is present in the individual. "Self-positive" is named so since it deals with what one can develop in oneself, over and above Self-competence and Social competence. The components of the Self-positive domain aim at self-enhancement, self-direction, and self-actualization. It involves the competencies of Authenticity, Positive Emotional Balance, Emotional Resilience, Self-compassion, Self-confidence, and Self-motivation.

"Emotional intelligence involves competencies related to understanding and managing one's own emotions, understanding others' emotions, developing and maintaining satisfying relationships with others and channelling one's emotional energy to create a positive self" (Anand, 2016).

The domain of Self-positive is the hallmark of all that emotional intelligence is and aims at. It involves achieving a balance between emotion and reason. It refers to using emotions to facilitate thought. The Self-positive domain aims at a new level where there is a congruence in emotion and action, bouncing back after adversity, being kind to oneself, experiencing more positive emotions, having a positive outlook in life, having confidence in oneself and using one's emotions to achieve goals. Hence, this is named as Self-positive.

The domain of Self-positive basically involves utilizing emotional energy to achieve a higher and positive self. Self-positive aims at using emotions in the best possible way. Let us discuss the various components of Self-positive.

a. Authenticity

Authenticity can be defined as a value orientation with respect to individuals, organizations, and communities. According to Berger and Luckmann (1967), "the authentic self is a constructed narrative, developed through interactions with significant others, and measured by the degree of congruence between the person's actual experience and their self-representation". Authentic selfhood is defined in terms of the "ideal self" towards which the individual strives and the clarity of the value commitments associated with that ideal (Taylor, 1989).

Authenticity is important not only from the point of the individual, but also for the society. Authenticity plays a key role in defining the normative framework of positive psychology.

Authenticity Describes a way of Being that Includes

- an orientation toward a 'higher' self
- freely chosen by the individual
- grounded in 'here and now' awareness
- helps in creating a coherent, and congruent self-narrative

Strategies for Developing Authenticity

- Having a sense of personal autonomy
- Persevering towards a higher self
- Being aware of the 'here and now'
- Keeping the bigger picture in mind
- Achieving congruence between one's experience and how it is represented in the self-system.
- Not unduly suppressing negative emotions and

finding healthy outlets for expressing them.

- Having confidence in oneself
- Having self-compassion and self-liking

b. Positive Emotional Balance

Human beings have the capacity to experience a wide range of emotions. We can feel emotions such as happiness, sadness, anger, frustration, surprise, disgust as well as also experience the combination of these emotions. People's emotional experience can be understood in terms of both positive and negative emotions. Positive emotions are joy, contentment, happiness, hope whereas negative emotions are anger, fear, sadness, disgust, guilt etc.

Emotional balance occurs when we try to feel our emotions as they occur, without being overwhelmed by them and accept our feelings without being judgmental. Positive Emotional Balance refers to trying to achieve a state where the balance of positive and negative emotions i.e. Positive Emotions-Negative Emotions is positive. This is desirable as positive emotions have many benefits.

Frederickson (1998, 2001) developed the Broaden and Build theory of positive emotions. According to this theory, positive emotions appear to broaden people's momentary thought-action repertoires and build their personal resources. Positive emotions widen the array of the thought-actions that come to mind.

Broadened mind-sets that accompany positive emotions have indirect and long-term adaptive benefits. These could be in terms of personal resources such as physical resources like health, longevity, social resources like social support networks, and intellectual resources like knowledge and psychological resources like resilience, creativity etc.

Due to the broaden and build effect, positive emotions create success and flourishing. People who frequently experience positive emotions have been found to be more happy and successful in their life. Positive emotions also lead to optimal functioning. Hence, positive emotions can be used intelligently to understand and guide one's behaviour and experience. There is also an adaptive significance of positive emotions.

According to Frederickson et al (2000), the undoing effect of positive emotions means that people can enhance their physical and psychological well-being by cultivating experience of positive emotions to cope with negative emotions. Hence, positive emotions act as a resource for coping with stress.

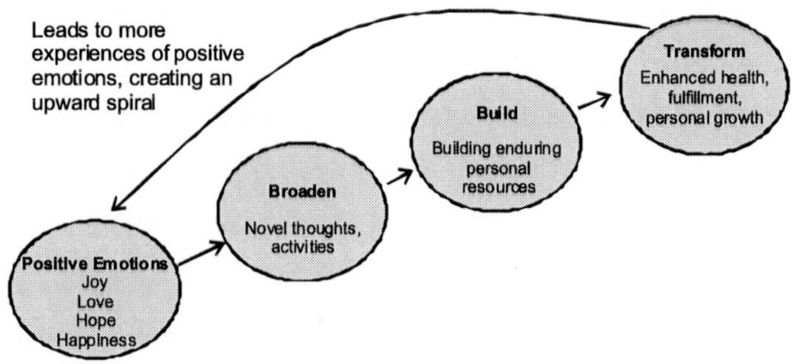

Figure 8.2 – Broaden-and-Build Theory of Positive Emotions

Adapted from Frederickson & Cohn (2008, Fig. 48.1)

Strategies for Achieving Positive Emotional Balance

- Being aware of the emotions one is experiencing
- Identifying the emotion being experienced
- Developing emotional regulation
- Enhancing distress tolerance
- Understanding the importance of positive emotions in our life
- Understanding that negative emotions are important too
- Trying to achieve a preponderance of positive emotions over negative emotions

c. Emotional Resilience

Emotional Resilience refers to one's ability to adapt to stressful situations and bouncing back from adversity due to some emotional trauma. Emotional Resilience also involves handling stress effectively.

Emotionally resilient people are high in emotional self-awareness. Therefore, they can identify what they are feeling and why they are feeling that way. Emotionally resilient people are perseverant and don't give up. They have an internal locus of control and believe that they are in control of themselves and that they have a choice in most situations. Emotionally resilient people are optimistic and are able to find supportive friends and family. They are able to manage distressing emotions.

Strategies for Developing Emotional Resilience

- Developing and maintaining close relationships.
- Looking at problems as challenges rather than as threats
- Accepting that change is a part of life.
- Being action oriented
- Setting challenging goals for oneself
- Self-discovery.
- Developing Self-compassion

d. Self-compassion

Compassion refers to being moved by the suffering of others and showing kindness to them. Compassion is considered to be a very important quality of being a human being. Often we talk about showing compassion towards others yet when it comes to our own self we are often very critical. Many times we focus more on our negative qualities, failures, and weaknesses and are very harsh on ourselves. Self-compassion involves being more accepting and kind towards oneself even though one is facing setbacks and failures. It involves not being judgmental or overly critical about oneself.

Self-compassion involves the understanding that failures and imperfection are a part of one's life. Therefore one has to be more accepting of this fact, and not be too hard on oneself. Self-compassion also requires looking at one's life in a larger perspective, and being more mindful.

Strategies for Developing Self-compassion

- Valuing oneself
- Being kind and accepting towards oneself
- Understanding that no one is perfect and every individual has strengths and weaknesses
- Not being too self-critical or judgmental
- Taking a balanced approach towards life

e. Self-confidence

Self-confidence is perhaps one of the most important characteristics of Self-positive. It refers to having confidence in oneself, having a belief in oneself to perform various activities, knowing oneself, and having a strong sense of self-worth. Self-confident individuals have self-assurance in their performance and success, are likely to take up new challenges, are straightforward, and are not pulled down by criticism. They have no unnecessary anxieties and worries and focus on the task at hand. They have the ability to confront any situation, are not afraid of criticism, and set challenging goals for themselves. They inspire others through their confidence, and are highly self-motivated.

A very important aspect of Self-confidence is assertiveness, which refers to the ability to assert, and show courage for saying or doing things in one's own way. It also involves communicating feelings and thoughts in a clear and appropriate way. Assertiveness helps in positive emotional management. This refers to managing emotions effectively, exercising control over emotions, and taking action without hurting the sentiments of others.

It also helps in building harmonious relationships through clear communication, and being considerate of others. One of the most important benefits of assertiveness is good physical and mental health achieved by minimizing unnecessary mental agonies, frustration, and hostility. Among supervisors, managers, and executives, a high degree of self-confidence distinguishes the best from the average performers (Boyatzis, 1982).

Strategies for Developing Self-confidence

- Developing a desire for self-confidence
- Developing self-knowledge
- Developing Emotional Self-awareness
- Developing Self-motivation
- Developing better decision making abilities
- Having appropriate role models
- Having self-acceptance

f. Self-motivation

Self-motivation is the most important aspect of Self-positive. Basically Self-motivation refers to having a sense of purpose and garnering resources to reach one's goals. This is quite related to intrinsic motivation.

A very important aspect of Self-motivation is *Achievement orientation.* Achievement orientation refers to an optimistic striving to continually improve performance. It involves working towards excellence; or a personal desire to do better than one did in the past or doing something better than others. People who are achievement oriented set high goals for themselves. They assess their performance objectively and look for better ways to improve their performance. Being achievement oriented involves anticipating risks or threats and working to overcome them. Achievement oriented individuals take time to think about how well they have done something and look for new and better ways to improve their skills and performance. They try to anticipate any difficulties in meeting their goals and take calculated risks if they need to in order to achieve what they want. Achievement orientation is a drive to accomplish one's goals and to meet or even surpass high standards of success. Achievement orientation involves taking full responsibility for one's actions, and decisions.

Another core component of Self-motivation is Optimism. Optimists expect good things to happen to them while pessimists expect bad things to happen to them. Dispositional optimism is defined as a global expectation that more good (desirable) things than bad (undesirable) will happen in the future (Scheier and Carver, 1985). Optimism has been found to be associated with greater life satisfaction whereas pessimism has been found to be associated with stress and depression. Dispositional Optimism is associated with various positive outcomes such as better mental and physical health, motivation, performance, and satisfying personal relationships. Optimism has been linked to positive mood, academic, and occupational success and good health. Pessimism has been found to be related to depression, failure, social isolation, mortality etc.

Since optimists are people who expect to have positive outcomes, they usually experience positive feelings. Pessimists expect negative outcomes and therefore they usually experience negative feelings of anxiety, guilt, anger etc. Seligman (1998) reported that optimistic people experience less depression and increased enjoyment in social interactions.

Optimistic people are healthier and happier. They cope better with stress using more effective coping strategies. They form better social support networks around themselves. They have healthier life-styles, which prevent them from developing illness. Working with Metropolitan Life Insurance Company, Seligman (1990) studied Optimism in insurance agents. He found that highly optimistic life insurance agents performed better than pessimists.

Strategies for Developing Self-motivation

- Identifying one's needs, motives, and goals
- Having appropriate role models to emulate
- Setting realistic yet challenging goals for oneself
- Having a desire to perform better than the last time
- Picking up activities one has always desired of doing
- Taking responsibility for oneself
- Looking for ways to inspire oneself
- Motivating oneself to achieve one's goals
- The approaches for changing pessimistic thinking to optimistic are all built on the same principles of "ABCDE" (Seligman, 1992).

A - Adverse event or situation- Identifying adverse situations that one routinely faces and writing down the objective descriptions of them.

B- Beliefs about that event- Learning to hear and record the beliefs about those events, which come to mind.

C - Consequences of those beliefs-Feeling the consequences of those beliefs and writing them down in terms of emotions and what one did.

D- Disputation and Distraction - Disputing those beliefs or distracting oneself.

E – Energization- Finally, noticing what happens to one's energy and willingness to act when one disputes the negative beliefs.

- Another method for enhancing Optimism is personal efficacy training. The focus of such training is on increasing specific kinds of competence by the use of assertiveness training or social skills training. Training in specific areas like problem solving, decision making can also improve the level of Optimism in a person.
- Looking back at happy memories and imagining happier events in the future
- Challenging negative self-talk
- Maintaining a positive outlook towards one's life

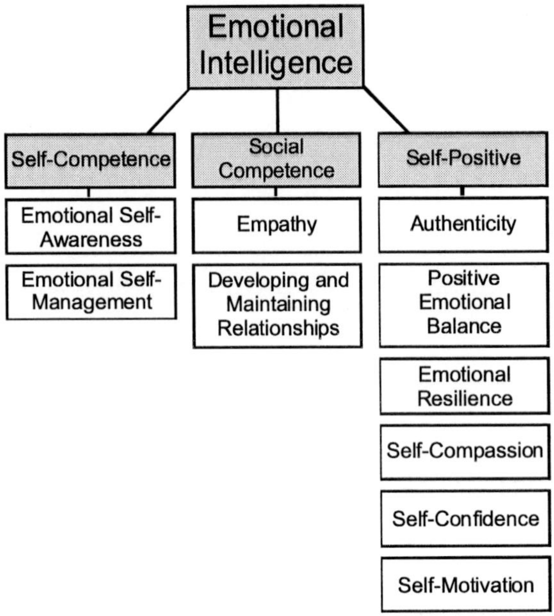

Figure 8.3 – 3S Model of Emotional Intelligence (Anand, 2016)

□□□

9

Emotional Intelligence: Need of the Hour

Human beings are emotional beings who experience emotions in varying levels of intensity. Therefore, understanding, expressing and managing emotions is of paramount importance in our personal lives and in interactions with others. Emotional intelligence presents a positive model for self-growth and development as well as experiencing satisfying relationships. It has implications for the ways people deal with their problems, physical and mental health, and for developing interventions for schools, organizations, and communities. Emotional intelligence involves various psychological mechanisms by which individuals flourish in their lives.

The world of today is characterized by globalization; fast pace of change and intense competition. All these challenges have led to an increase in stress, anxiety and depression. Everyday news is full of reports of increase in aggressive and violent acts. We routinely come across reports of acts of violence occurring in homes, neighborhoods and at schools. The destruction caused by these aggressive and violent acts is tremendous. The past decade has witnessed a sharp rise in the incidents of violence. There is an increase in crime against women and children, bullying at school and workplace, drug addiction and suicide, which reflect the diminishing social values existing in our families and the society at large. Juvenile violence has become prominent in schools worldwide and in India in particular. The recent killings in schools by students in the last few years have shaken the very roots of Indian society. Road rage has become quite common today. What is most disturbing is the fact that a very high percentage of the offenders are below the age of 25.

These problems are rooted in emotional mismanagement and poor emotional skills. These incidents clearly reveal the fact that somewhere our educational system and family upbringing have failed to develop empathy and compassion in the young generation. "There is a worldwide trend for the present generation to be more troubled emotionally than the last, more lonely and depressed, more angry and unruly, more nervous and more prone to worry, more impulsive and aggressive" (Goleman, 1995).

The World Health Organization in its factsheet on depression (2016) has stated that depression is the leading cause of disability worldwide, and is a major contributor to the overall global burden of disease. Also it has been found that the majority of stress-related problems occur due to abusive and unsatisfying relationships.

Therefore, the most serious question before us is how to tackle the growing menace of aggression and violence, stress, drug abuse and other emerging problems. The answer is through emotional intelligence. Emotional intelligence as a concept has become all the more significant today as the society is going through massive changes. There is a desperate need for training in managing emotions to deal with difficult situations since emotional intelligence includes abilities such as self-control, empathy and the ability to motivate oneself and create a positive self.

In our society there is a lot of emphasis on IQ and academic achievement. But there have been many studies that show that IQ is not the only factor important for success. Our emotional intelligence has a large impact on our success in life and therefore it is important that we fully develop our emotional skills. Yet there is very little emphasis on emotional intelligence.

Hence, given the importance of emotional intelligence in today's world, it is crucial that concrete steps are taken towards enhancing emotional intelligence in people. Many countries across the world have started making efforts in this direction. More and more efforts are required in our country too. Efforts should be aimed at incorporating emotional intelligence in the school and college curriculum as well so that children are taught right from the beginning about the importance of understanding and managing their emotions. Awareness programmes must be created to make everyone aware about the importance of emotional intelligence. Training programmes must be organized at the organizational level too so that the employees are trained in the competencies of emotional intelligence.

All this requires integrated efforts and cooperation from individuals from all walks of life whether it is parents, teachers, administrators or leaders. Hence, everyone must come together and make efforts towards enhancing emotional intelligence so that individuals are better adept at understanding and managing their emotions. In this way we all can come together and make the world a better place!

□□□

References

Allport, F. H. (1924). *Social Psychology*. Boston: Houghton Mifflin.

Anand, P. V. (2013). Emotional intelligence and self-efficacy as predictors of life satisfaction among undergraduate students. *Journal of Positive Psychology, 2* (1), 34-49.

Anand, P. V. (2015, February). *Happiness in young adults: The role of gratitude, emotional intelligence, and forgiveness*. Paper presented at 3rd National and First International Conference of Positive Psychology organized by the Indian Association of Positive Psychology at Manav Rachna International University, Faridabad.

Anand, P. V. (2015). Enhancing emotional intelligence: An intervention based study. *Journal of Positive Psychology, 4* (1, 2), 5-16.

Asch, S. E. (1952). *Social Psychology*. New Jersey: Prentice Hall, Inc.

Ashforth, B., & Humphrey, R. (1995). Emotion in the workplace - a reappraisal. *Human Relations, 48*, 97- 125.

Ashkanasy, N. M., & Dasborough, M. T. (2003). Emotional awareness and emotional intelligence in leadership teaching. *Journal of Education for Business, 79*, 18-22.

Barling, J., Slater, F. & Kelloway, E. K. (2000). Transformational leadership and emotional intelligence: an exploratory study. *Leadership and Organizational Development Journal, 21*, 157-61.

Bar-On, R. (1997). *Bar-On Emotional Quotient Inventory (EQ-I): Technical Manual.* Toronto, Canada: Multi-Health Systems.

Bar-On, R. (2000). Emotional and social intelligence: Insights from the Emotional Quotient Inventory (EQ-i). In R. Bar-On & J. D. A. Parker (Eds.), *Handbook of emotional intelligence*. San Francisco: Jossey-Bass.

Bar-On, R. (2012). The impact of emotional intelligence on health and wellbeing, emotional intelligence - New perspectives and applications, Prof. Annamaria Di Fabio (Ed.), InTech, DOI: 10.5772/32468. Retrieved from: http://www.intechopen.com/books/emotional-intelligence-new-perspectives-and-applications/the-impact-of-emotional-intelligence-on-health-and-wellbeing.

Bar-On, R., Handley, R., & Fund, S. (2005). The impact of emotional and social intelligence on performance. In Vanessa Druskat, Fabio Sala, and Gerald Mount (Eds.), *Linking emotional intelligence and performance at work: Current research evidence*. Mahwah, NJ: Lawrence Erlbaum.

Bar-On, R., & Parker, J. D. A. (Eds.) (2000). *The handbook of emotional intelligence*. San Francisco, California: Jossey Bros.

Berger, P. L. & Luckmann, T. (1967). *The social construction of reality: a treatise in the sociology of knowledge.* Penguin, Harmondsworth (Original: Doubleday. Garden City, N. Y. 1966).

Bhalla, S. & Nauriyal, D. K. (2004). Emotional intelligence: The emerging paradigm in personnel dynamics. *Psychological Studies, 49* (2 & 3), 97-106.

Bhattacharya, M., Dutta, A. K., & Mandal M. K. (2004). Factor structure of emotional intelligence in India. *Psychological Studies, 49* (2 & 3), 142-146.

Boyatzis, R. E. (1982). *The competent manager: A model of effective performance*. New York: Wiley.

Boyatzis, R. E. (1999). *The financial impact of competencies in leadership and management of consulting firms*. Department of Organizational Behavior Working Paper, Case Western Reserve University, Cleveland.

Boyatzis, R. E., Goleman, D. & Rhee, K. (2000). Clustering competence in emotional intelligence: Insights from the Emotional Competence Inventory (ECI). In R. Bar-On and J.D.A. Parker (eds.), *Handbook of emotional intelligence* (pp. 343-362). San Francisco: Jossey-Bass.

Brackett, M. A. &Katulak, N. A. (2006). Emotional intelligence in the classroom: A skill-based training for teachers and students. In J. Ciarrochi& J. D. Mayer (Eds.), *Improving Emotional Intelligence: A Practitioner's Guide* (pp.1.27). New York: Psychology Press.

Brackett, M. A. & Mayer, J. D. (2003). Convergent, discriminant, and incremental validity of competing measures of emotional intelligence. *Personality and Social Psychology Bulletin, 29*(9), 1147-1158.

Brackett, M. A., Palomera, R., Mojsa-kaja, J., Reyes, M. R., & Salovey, P. (2010). Emotion-regulation ability, burnout, and job satisfaction among British secondary-school teachers. *Psychology in the Schools, 47*, 406–417.

Bradberry, J. & Greaves, J. (2009). *Emotional intelligence 2.0*. San Diego, CA: Talent Smart.

Cannon, W. B. (1927). The James-Lange theory of emotions: A critical examination and an alternative theory. *The American Journal of Psychology, 39,* 106–124.

Cherniss, C. (2000, April). *Emotional intelligence: What it is and why it matters?* Paper presented at the Annual Meeting of the Society for Industrial and Organizational Psychology, New Orleans.

Ciarrochi, J. V. Chan, A. Y. C. &Caputi, P. (2000). A critical evaluation of the emotional intelligence construct. *Personality and Individual Differences, 28,* 539-561.

Damasio, A. R. (1994). *Descartes' Error: Emotion, Reason and the Human Brain.* Papermac, London.

Darwin, C. (1965). *The expression of the emotions in man and animals.* Chicago: University of Chicago Press. (Original work published 1872).

Davies, M., Stankov, L. & Roberts, R. D. (1998). Emotional intelligence: in search of an elusive construct. *Journal of Personality and Social Psychology, 75,* 989-1015.

Dawda, R. & Hart, S. D. (2000). Assessing emotional intelligence: Reliability and validity of the Bar-On Emotional Quotient Inventory (EQ-i) in university students. *Personality and Individual Differences, 28*(4), 797–812.

Downey, L. A., Mountstephen, J., Lloyd, J., Hansen, K., &Stough, C. (2008). Emotional intelligence and scholastic achievement in Australian adolescents. *Australian Journal of Psychology, 60*(1), 10–17.

Dulewicz, V. & Higgs, M. (2001). *The development of a 360 degree Emotional Intelligence questionnaire for the general working population.* Henley Working Paper Series. 01/01.

Durlak, J. A., Weissberg, R. P., Dymnicki, A. B., Taylor, R. D., &Schellinger, K. B. (2011). The impact of enhancing students' social and emotional learning: A meta-analysis of school-based universal interventions. *Child Development,* 82: 405–432.

Ekman, P. (1992). Facial expressions of emotion: New findings, new questions. *Psychological Science, 3*(1), 34-38.

Ekman, P., & Friesen, W. V. (1971). Constants across culture in the face and emotion. *Journal of Personality and Social Psychology, 17,* 124-129.

Ekman, P., Friesen, W. V., & Ellsworth, P. (1972). *Emotion in the human face: guide-lines for research and an integration of findings.* New York: Pergamon Press.

Ellis, A. (1962). *Reason and emotion in psychotherapy.* New York: Lyle Stuart.

Fredrickson, B. L. (1998). What good are positive emotions? *Review of General Psychology, 2,* 300–319.

Fredrickson, B. L. (2001). The role of positive emotions in positive psychology: The broaden-and-build theory of positive emotion. *American Psychologist, 56,* 218-226.

Fredrickson, B. L., & Cohn, M. A. (2008). Positive emotions. In M. Lewis, J. Haviland-Jones & L. F. Barrett (Eds.), *Handbook of emotions* (pp. 777–796). (3rd ed.). New York: Guilford Press.

Friesen, W. V. (1972). *Cultural differences in facial expressions in a social situation: An experimental test of the concept of display rules.* Doctoral dissertation, University of California, San Francisco.

Ganesan, S. (1993). Negotiation strategies and the nature of channel relationship. *Journal of marketing research, 30*(2), 183–203.

Gardner, H. (1983). *Frames of mind.* New York: Basic Books.

Gardner, H. (1993). *Multiple Intelligences*. New York: Basic Books.

Gibbs, N. (1995, October 2). What's your EQ? *Time,* pp. 60-68.

Gohm, C. L., Corser, G. C., & Dalsky, D. J. (2005). Emotional intelligence under stress: Useful, unnecessary, or irrelevant? *Personality and Individual Differences, 39*(6), 1017–1028.

Goleman, D. (1995). *Emotional Intelligence*. New York: Bantam Book.

Goleman, D. (1998). *Working with Emotional Intelligence*. New York: Bantam Books.

Goleman, D. (2000). Emotional intelligence: Issues in paradigm building. In D. Goleman, & C. Cherniss (eds.), *The Emotionally Intelligent Workplace: How to Select for, Measure, and Improve Emotional Intelligence in Individuals, Groups, and Organizations*. San Francisco, CA: Jossey-Bass.

Goleman, D. (2001). Emotional intelligence: Issues in paradigm building. In C. Cherniss & D. Goleman (Eds.), *The emotionally intelligent workplace,* (pp. 13-26), Jossey-Bass: San Francisco.

Goleman, D., Boyatzis, R. E., & Rhee, K. S. (2000). Clustering competence in emotional intelligence: Insights from the emotional competence inventory. In R. Bar-On and J.D.A. Parker (Eds.), *Handbook of emotional intelligence* (pp. 343-362). San Francisco: Jossey-Bass.

Groves, K. S., McEnrue, M. P, & Shen, W. (2008). Developing and measuring the emotional intelligence of leaders. *Journal of Management Development, 27*(2), 225-250.

Handley. R. (1997, April). AFRS rates emotional intelligence. *Air Force Recruiter News*.

Hay/McBer Research and Innovation Group (1997). In D. Goleman

(1998), *Working with Emotional Intelligence*. New York: Bantam Books.

Hay/McBer (2000). *Research into teacher effectiveness: a model of teacher effectiveness*. Report by Hay McBer to the Department for Education & Employment. London: DfEE.

Hemphill, J. K. (1955). Leadership behavior associated with the administrative reputation of college departments. *Journal of Educational Psychology, 46,* 385–401.

Hemphill, J. K. (1959). Job description for executives. *Harvard Business Review, 37*(5), 55-67.

Izard, C. E. (1989). The structure and functions of emotions: Implications for cognition, motivation, and personality. In I. S. Cohen (Ed.), *The G. Stanley Hall Lecture Series (Vol. 9, pp. 35-73).* Washington, DC: American Psychological Association.

James, W. (1879). Are we automata? *Mind, 4,* 1-22.

James, W. (1950). *Principles of psychology* (Vol.2). New York: Dover. (Original work published 1890)

Jdaitawi, M. T., Ishak, N. A., Tamneh, M. A., Gharaibeh, M. N., Rababah, L. M. (2011). The effectiveness of emotional intelligence training program on social and academic adjustment among first year university students. *International Journal of Business and Social Science, 24* (2), 251-258.

Jordan, P. J. & Troth, A. C. (2004). Managing emotions during team problem solving: emotional intelligence and conflict resolution. *Human Performance, 17,* 195-218.

Joseph, D. L., & Newman, D. A. (2010). Emotional intelligence: An integrative meta-analysis and cascading model. *Journal of Applied Psychology, 95,* 54–78.

Kirk, B. A., Schutte, N. S., & Hine, D. W. (2011). The effect of an expressive writing intervention for employees on emotional self-efficacy, emotional intelligence, affect, and workplace incivility. *Journal of Applied Social Psychology, 41, 179-195.*

Lazarus, R. S. (2001). Relational meaning and discrete emotions. In K. Scherer, A. Schorr, & T. Johnstone (Eds.), *Appraisal processes in emotion: Theory, methods, research (pp. 37–67).* New York: Oxford University Press.

Lopes, P. N., Salovey, P., & Straus, R. (2003). Emotional intelligence, personality, and the perceived quality of social relationships. *Personality and Individual Differences, 35,* 641–658.

Lusch, R. F., & Serpkeuci, R. (1990). Personal differences, job tension, job outcomes, and store performance: A study of retail managers. *Journal of Marketing*, 54, 85-101.

Mahoney, M. J., (1991). *Human change processes: The scientific foundations of psychotherapy.* New York: Basic Books.

Malouff, J. M, Schutte, N. S., & Thorsteinsson, E. (2014). Trait emotional intelligence and romantic relationship satisfaction: A meta-analysis. *American Journal of Family Therapy, 42,* 53–66.

Martins, A., Ramalho, N., & Morin, E. (2010). A comprehensive meta-analysis of the relationship between emotional intelligence and health. *Personality and Individual Differences, 49* (6), 554–564.

Mayer, J. D., Caruso, D. R., & Salovey, P. (1999). Emotional intelligence meets traditional standards for an intelligence. *Intelligence, 27,* 267– 298.

Mayer, J. D., & Geher, G. (1996). Emotional intelligence and the identification of emotion. *Intelligence, 22,* 89-113.

Mayer, J. D., & Salovey, P. (1993). The intelligence of emotional intelligence. *Intelligence, 17,* 433–442.

Mayer, J. D., & Salovey, P. (1995). Emotional intelligence and the construction and regulation of feelings. *Applied and Preventive Psychology, 4,* 197-208.

Mayer, J. D., & Salovey, P. (1997). What is emotional intelligence? In P. Salovey & D. J. Sluyter (Eds.) *Emotional Development and Emotional Intelligence*. New York: Basic Books.

Mayer, J. D., Salovey, P., & Caruso, D. R. (2000). Models of emotional intelligence. In R. J. Sternberg (Ed.), *The handbook of intelligence* (pp. 396–420). New York: Cambridge University Press.

Mayer, J. D., Salovey, P., & Caruso, D. (2002). *MSCEIT User's Manual*. Toronto, ON: Multi-Health Systems.

Mayer, J. D., Salovey, P., & Caruso, D. R. (2004). Emotional intelligence: Theory, findings, and implications. *Psychological Inquiry, 60,* 197– 215.

Mayer, J. D., Salovey P., Caruso, D. R.& Sitarenios, G. (2001). Emotional intelligence as a standard intelligence. *Emotion, 1,* 232–42.

McClelland, D. C. (1973). Testing for competence rather than for "intelligence." *American Psychologist, 28,* 1-14.

McClelland, D. C. (1998). Identifying competencies with behavioral-event interviews. *Psychological Science, 9*(5), 331-340.

Mowrer, O. H. (1960). *Learning theory and behavior.* New York: John Wiley and sons.

Nelis, D., Kotsou, I., Quoidbach, J., Hansenne, M., Weytens, F., Dupuis, P., & Mikolajczak, M. (2011). Increasing emotional competence improves psychological and physical well-being, social relationships, and employability. *Emotion, 11,* 354-366.

O'Boyle, E. H., Humphrey, R. H., Pollack, J. M., Hawver, T. H., & Story, P. A. (2011). The relation between emotional intelligence and job performance: A meta-analysis. *Journal of Organizational Behavior, 32,* 788-818.

Office of Strategic Services Assessment Staff. (1948). *Assessment of men*. New York: Rinehart.

Orioli, E. M., Jones, T. & Trocki, K. H. (1999). *EQ Map Technical Manual.* San Francisco, CA: Q-Metrics.

Pandey, R., & Tripathi, A. N., (2004). Development of emotional intelligence: Some preliminary observations. *Psychological Studies, 49* (2 & 3), 147-150.

Panksepp, J. (2005). Affective consciousness: Core emotional feelings in animals and humans. *Consciousness and Cognition, 14,* 30–80.

Pant, N. & Prakash, A., (2004). Multi-factor Emotional Intelligence Scale (MEIS) in India: An evaluation. *Psychological Studies, 49 (2 & 3),* 128-135.

Parker, J. D. A., Taylor, G. J., & Bagby, R. M. (2001). The relationship between emotional intelligence and alexithymia. *Personality and Individual Differences, 30,* 107–115.

Passer, M. W. & Smith, R. E. (2011). *Psychology: The Science of Mind and Behavior. (5th ed.).* New York: McGraw-Hill.

Patti, J., Senge, P., Madrazo, C., & Stern, R. (2015). Developing socially, emotionally, and cognitively competent school leaders and learning communities. In J. A. Durlak, C. E. Domitrovich, R. P. Weissberg & T. P. Gullotta (Eds.), *Handbook of social and emotional learning: Research and practice.* New York, NY: Guilford Press.

Payne, W. L. (1983/1986). A study of emotion: developing emotional intelligence; Self integration; relating to fear, pain and desire. *Dissertation Abstracts International, 47,* 203A.

Pesuric, A., & Byham, W. (1996). The new look in behavior modeling. *Training and Development,* 25-33.

Petrides, K. V., Frederickson, N., & Furnham, A. (2004). The role of trait emotional intelligence in academic performance and deviant behavior at school. *Personality and Individual Differences, 36,* 277–293.

Petrides, K. V. & Furnham, A. (2000). Gender differences in measured and self-estimated trait emotional intelligence. *Sex Roles, 42,* (5/6), 449-461.

Petrides, K.V., Pérez-González, J. C., & Furnham, A. (2007). On the criterion and incremental validity of trait emotional intelligence. *Cognition and Emotion, 21*(1), 26-55.

Plutchik, R. (1994). *The Psychology and Biology of Emotion.* New York, NY: Harper Collins College Publishers.

Pragadeeswaran, S. & Panchanatham, N. (2003). Need for effective training to enhance emotional quotient for business executives. *Indian Journal of Training and Development. 33*(384), 143-148.

Reuben, E., P. Sapienza, & Zingales, L. (2009). Is mistrust self-fulfilling? *Economics Letters, 104,* 89-91.

Rivers, S. E., Brackett, M. A., Reyes, M. R., Elbertson, N. A., &Salovey, P. (2013). Improving the social and emotional climate of classroms: A clustered randomized controlled trial testing The RULER Approach. *Prevention Science, 14,* 77-87.

Ruderman, M. N., Hannum, K., Leslie, J. B., & Steed, J. (2001). Making the connection: leadership skills and emotional intelligence. *Leadership in Action, 21*(5), 3-7.

Ruiz-Aranda, D., Castillo, R., Salquero, J. M., Cabello, R., Fernandez-Berrocal, P., & Balluerka, N. (2012). Short and midterm effects of emotional intelligence training on adolescent mental health. *Journal of Adolescent Health, 51,* 462-467.

Saarni, C. (1999). The development of emotional competence. New York: Guilford.

Saarni, C. (2000). Emotional competence: A developmental perspective. In Bar-On, R., J.D.A. Parker (eds.), *The Handbook of Emotional Intelligence* (pp. 68-91). Jossey-Bass: San Francisco.

Saarni, C. (2001). Cognition, context, and goals: Significant components in social-emotional effectiveness. *Social Development, 10,* 125–129.

Salovey, P. & Mayer, J. D. (1990). Emotional Intelligence. *Imagination, Cognition and Personality, 9,* 185-211.

Salovey, P., Mayer, J. D., Goldman, S. L., Turvey, C., & Palfai, T. P. (1995). Emotional attention, clarity, and repair: Exploring emotional intelligence using the trait meta-mood scale. In J. Pennebaker (Ed.), *Emotion, disclosure, & health* (pp. 125–154). Washington, DC: American Psychological Association.

Schachter, S. (1966). The interaction of cognitive and physiological determinants of emotional state. In C. D. Spielberger (Ed.), *Anxiety and behavior*. New York: Academic Press.

Scheier, M. F., & Carver, C. S. (1985). Optimism, coping, and health: Assessment and implications of generalized outcome expectancies. *Health Psychology, 4,* 219-247.

Scheier, M. F., Magovern, G. J., Abbott, R. A., Matthews, K. L., Owens, J. F., Lefebvre, R. C. & Carver, C. S. (1989). Dispositional optimism and recovery from coronary artery bypass surgery: The beneficial effects on physical and psychological well-being. *Journal of Personality and Social Psychology, 57,* 1024-1040.

Schutte, N. S. & Malouff, J. M. (2002). Incorporating emotional skills in a college transition course enhances student retention. *Journal of the First-Year Experience and Students in Transition, 14,* 7-21.

Schutte, N. S., Malouff, J. M., Hall, L. E., Haggerty, D. J., Cooper, J. T., Golden, C. H. & Dornheim, L. (1998). Development and validation of a measure of emotional intelligence. *Personality and Individual Difference, 25,* 167-177.

Schutte, N. S., Malouff, J. M., Thorsteinsson, E. B., Bhullar, N. & Rooke, S. E. (2007) A meta-analytic investigation of the relationship between emotional intelligence and health. *Personality and Individual Differences 42*(6), 921-933.

Seligman, M. E. P. (1990). *Learned optimism.* New York: Knopf.

Seligman, M. E. P. (1992). *Learned optimism: how to change your mind and your life.* New York: Pocket Books.

Seligman, M. E. P. (1998). Positive social science. *APA Monitor, 29*(4), 2, 5.

Shanwal, V. K. (2004). *Emotional Intelligence: The Indian Scenario.* Indian Publishers Distributors.

Shoda, Y., Mischel, W., & Peake, P. K. (1990). Predicting adolescent cognitive and self-regulatory competencies from preschool delay of gratification: Identifying diagnostic conditions. *Developmental Psychology, 26(6),* 978-986.

Sibia, A., Misra, G., & Srivastava A. K., (2005). Assessing emotional intelligence in the Indian context. *Psychological Studies, 50(2 & 3*), 263-271.

Singh, D. (2001). *Emotional intelligence at work: A professional guide*. New Delhi: Sage.

Singh, D. & Chadha, N. K. (2001). How to measure your EQ. In D. Singh (Ed.), *Emotional intelligence at work: A professional guide*. New Delhi: Sage.

Singh, S. (2004). Development of a measure of emotional intelligence. *Psychological Studies, 49,* 136-141.

Sivanathan, N., & Fekken, G. C. (2002). Emotional intelligence and transformational leadership. *Leadership and Organization Development Journal, 23,* 198-204.

Slaski, M., & Cartwright, S. (2002). Health, performance and emotional intelligence: An exploratory study of retail managers. *Stress and Health, 18,* 63-68.

Slaski, M., & Cartwright, S. (2003). Emotional intelligence training and its implications for stress, health, and performance. *Stress and Health, 19,* 233-239.

Spencer, L. M. (1997). Competency assessment methods. In L. J. Bassi& Russ-Eft (Eds.), *What works: Assessment, Development, and Measurement*. Alexandria, VA: American Society for Training and Development.

Spencer, L. M. J., McClelland, D. C., &Kelner, S. (1997). *Competency assessment methods: History and state of the art*. Boston: Hay/

McBer.

Spencer, L. M., Jr., & Spencer, S. (1993). *Competence at work: Models for superior performance*. New York: John Wiley and Sons.

Spinoza, B. (1677/1989). *Ethica*. (translated by G.H.R. Parkinson). London: Everyman.

Srivastava, K. B. L. & Bharamanaikar, S. R. (2004). Emotional intelligence and effective leadership behavior. *Psychological Studies, 49* (2 & 3), 107-113.

Sternberg, R. J. (1985). *Beyond IQ: A Triarchic Theory of Intelligence.* Cambridge: Cambridge University Press.

Sternberg, R. J. (1991). Theory-based testing of intellectual abilities: Rationale for the Triarchic Abilities Test. In H. Rowe (Eds.), *Intelligence: Reconceptualization and measurement* (pp. 183-202). Hillsdale, NJ: Lawrence Erlbaum.

Sternberg, R. J., Wagner, R. K., Williams, W. M., & Horvath, J. A. (1995). Testing common sense. *American Psychologist, 50*(11), 912-927.

Suveg, C., & Zeman, J. (2004). Emotion regulation in children with anxiety disorders. *Journal of Clinical Child and Adolescent Psychology, 33,* 750-759.

Swift, D. G. (2002). *The relationship of emotional intelligence, hostility, and anger to heterosexual male intimate partner violence*. New York University, New York, NY.

Taylor, C. (1989). *Sources of the Self: The making of the modern identity.* Cambridge, MA: Harvard University Press.

Thingujam, N. K. S., & Ram, U. (1999, December). *Indian norms of*

Emotional Intelligence Scale and some correlates. Paper Presented at 5th International and 36th IAAP Applied Psychology Conference.

Thingujan, N. K.S. & Ram, U. (2000). Emotional intelligence scale: Indian norms. *Journal of Education and Psychology, 58,* 40-48.

Thorndike, E. L. (1920). Intelligence and its use. *Harper's Magazine, 140,* 227-235.

Tomkins, S. S. (1962). *Affect, Imagery, Consciousness, Volume 1, The Positive Affects.* New York: Springer.

Tomkins, S. S. (1963). *Affect, Imagery, Consciousness, Volume 2, The Negative Affects.* New York: Springer.

Trinidad, D. R., Johnson, C. A. (2002). The association between emotional intelligence and early adolescent tobacco and alcohol use. *Personality and Individual Differences. 32*(1), 95-105.

Van Rooy, D. L., Viswesvaran, C., & Pluta, P. (2005). An evaluation of construct validity: What is this thing called emotional intelligence? *Human Performance, 18,* 445–462.

Wechsler, D. (1944). *The measurement of adult intelligence (3rd ed.).* Baltimore: Williams & Wilkins.

Williams, D. (1994). *Leadership for the 21st Century: Life Insurance Leadership Study.* Boston: Hay Group.

Yrizarry, N., Matsumoto, D., Imai, C., Kooken, K., & Takeuchi, S. (2001). Culture and emotion. In L. L. Adler & U. P Gielen (Eds.), *Cross-cultural topics in Psychology (2nd ed.).* Westport, CT: Praeger.

Zijlmans, L. J. M., Embregts, P. J. C. M., Gerits, L., Bosman, A. M. T., &Derksen, J. J. L. (2011). Training emotional intelligence related to treatment skills of staff working with clients with intellectual disabilities and challenging behaviour. *Journal of Intellectual Disability Research, 55,* 219-230.